More Praise for *Digital Relevance*

"Ardath Albee has a unique talent for blowing away the hype and hyper-bole that plagues digital marketing. *Digital Relevance* is an important book because it's a bright, clear call to specific action. It's packed with authority and practical strategies and told with energy and attitude."

—Doug Kessler, Creative Director and Co-Founder, Velocity

"Ardath has published the solution to the very real problem in marketing today: how can our content be better aligned with our business objectives? She titled it *Digital Relevance*. But she could've titled it Digital Marketing Reset."

—Ann Handley, Chief Content Officer, MarketingProfs and author of *Everybody Writes*

"This book demonstrates how lack of strategy and customer orientation are putting a strain on marketers and on our ability to produce real business results. In order to achieve a connection with our future customers, we need to create content that delivers value and meaning in a targeted way. And *Digital Relevance* shows us how."

—Michael Brenner, Head of Strategy, NewsCred

"There's a revolution coming in the B2B marketing world and on the front line is the dynamic marketer. In *Digital Relevance*, Ardath Albee delivers her message of relevance, context, and connection in one of the best books on content marketing I've ever read. Buy and know this book before your competition does."

—Lee Odden, CEO, TopRankMarketing.com and author of *OptimizeBook.com*

"Content marketing is no longer a game of numbers; it's now a game of relevance. If there was a such thing as a Ph.D in content relevance, Ardath Albee would have just delivered the required reading."

—Jason Miller, Sr. Content Marketing Manager, LinkedIn

"*Digital Relevance* is a necessary reading for every marketer who believes content matter—and especially for those who don't! Ardath provides an encompassing structure with many detailed examples of how content should be considered, created, executed, and measured. This is a how-to book for every marketer wanting to understand both the tactics and the strategy of content marketing. But be warned: Ardath will challenge the way you think about content and campaigns!"

—Debbie Qaqish, Chief Strategy Officer,
The Pedowitz Group

Digital Relevance

Developing Marketing Content and Strategies that Drive Results

Ardath Albee

DIGITAL RELEVANCE
Copyright © Marketing Interactions, Inc. 2015.

First published in 2015 by
PALGRAVE MACMILLAN®
in the United States—a division of St. Martin's Press LLC,
175 Fifth Avenue, New York, NY 10010.

Where this book is distributed in the UK, Europe and the rest of the world,
this is by Palgrave Macmillan, a division of Macmillan Publishers Limited,
registered in England, company number 785998, of Houndmills,
Basingstoke, Hampshire RG21 6XS.

Palgrave Macmillan is the global academic imprint of the above companies
and has companies and representatives throughout the world.

Palgrave® and Macmillan® are registered trademarks in the United States,
the United Kingdom, Europe and other countries.

ISBN: 978–1–137–45280–1

Library of Congress Cataloging-in-Publication Data

Albee, Ardath.
    Digital relevance : developing marketing content and strategies
  that drive results / Ardath Albee.
      pages cm
    ISBN 978–1–137–45280–1 (hardback)—
    ISBN 1–137–45280–3
    1. Marketing. 2. Strategic planning. 3. Customer relations.
  4. Selling—Computer network resources. I. Title.

HF5415.A374 2015
658.8'72—dc23   2014027486

A catalogue record of the book is available from the British Library.

Design by Newgen Knowledge Works (P) Ltd., Chennai, India.

First edition: January 2015

10 9 8 7 6 5 4 3 2 1

Printed in the United States of America.

To my father, who always told me I was "a woman of vast potential," my mom, who made sure I had every opportunity, and my husband, Lou, who makes it real every day by encouraging me to go for it, even when it seems impossible.

Contents

Figures

Acknowledgments

The motivation for this book came from my very good friend and sales strategist extraordinaire, Jill Konrath, who convinced me that I'd learned enough through my project work since my last book to write a new one. She was right. Thanks to my agent, John Willig, who jumped on board and helped me refine the concept and take it to market. I'm grateful to my editor, Laurie Harting, for her feedback on where to expand concepts and her encouragement for the storytelling aspects I've included in the book. She's truly a joy to work with, as is her patient editorial assistant, Alexis Nelson.

Mostly, I'd like to thank my clients for believing in my strategies—sometimes as a leap of faith—taking them to market, incorporating your expertise, and accomplishing great outcomes for your organizations. It's my pleasure to work with you every day.

In addition, I'd like to acknowledge a few people with whom I've had great debates, brainstorming, and idea sessions while developing many of the ideas in the book. The list is far more extensive than this and I apologize for anyone I've failed to include. In no particular order, I'm blessed to know Rebel Brown, Carlos Hidalgo, Matt Heinz, Robert Rose, Joe Pulizzi, Michael Brenner, Jason Stewart, Susyn Elise Duris, Michele Linn, Dan McDade, Jeff Ernst, Glenn Conradt, Lee Odden, Kirsten Jepson, Nick Sellers, Craig Rosenberg, Sherri Whittington, John Cousineau, and Carla Johnson.

Finally, thanks to my husband, Lou, for encouraging the madness that comes with writing a book while carrying a full project load. I'm sure it must look like chaos from where you're sitting. Thanks for taking the ride with me!

Introduction

A few years ago, I spent a lot of time convincing marketers about the value of investing in content marketing. Today, I get calls from marketers saying, *"We bought into the idea of content marketing. We've created great content. People read it. But it's not moving the needle."*

When I go online to take a look to offer feedback and advice, I usually see decent content. What I don't see is any strategic plan for orchestrating engagement with prospects and customers. I don't see any attempt at relationship building. Mostly, I see areas for improvement in relevance, context, and connection. This is because companies tend to talk about what they know best—their products. Even when marketers think they're developing content for buyers, they're not—not really. The problem remains that they don't know their buyers well enough to provide the level of valuable information mixed with an emotional connection that buyers are searching for. Quite often, they also don't know their customers very well. But compounding the issue is a one-off mind-set that inhibits storytelling over the length of the buying process. Rectifying these issues gets to the heart of context and relevance.

I wrote *Digital Relevance* for the marketers, corporate communications professionals, consultants, and entrepreneurs faced with the need to build relationships with elusive buyers whose context can change in a nanosecond. Technology was billed as the answer. But it's only confused the issue because the strategy is lacking. Marketing has changed—and changed fast—leaving marketers adrift without the foundation, mind-set, and skills they need to master the dynamics of digital engagement when faced with shrinking attention spans and the increasing noise and velocity of content publishing. Meanwhile, the pressure for accountability builds every day with marketers unsure how to prove what they do matters. Yet matter it does.

To be successful, marketers must implement highly personalized and integrated programs today in channels and manners they haven't ever used before. The breadth of skills required to succeed in marketing has increased dramatically. For marketers used to coordinating the activities of external agencies and focusing on one stand-alone campaign at a time, a large gap in competency has been exposed.

Filling this gap will require that marketers develop customer-oriented communications, identify the distinct value that differentiates their company, make the shift from one-off communications to a continuum approach, and ensure that data and metrics are used to relate their programs to the achievement of business objectives.

More than $40 billion is spent globally each year producing and using custom content in marketing programs. But how much of that money is bringing quantifiable return on investment? How long will companies continue to spend on marketing programs that don't help achieve business objectives?

Publishing content without a strategy isn't moving the needle. Time, effort, and money are flushed away without a quantifiable impact on business performance. This is a serious problem for marketers. Their companies expect results. Their jobs are on the line. If not now, then soon.

Many of the marketers I speak with are concerned that their marketing isn't as effective as it could be. They know that buyers and customers prefer digital information and communications, but they're not confident in how to go about creating relevant content successfully. And, they're deeply concerned that they won't be able to reach their customers as the competition for attention online increases. Much of the marketing content I see lacks the personalization and targeting that is needed to do more than engage prospects or customers briefly, in the immediate moment.

This just won't do. Buyers have changed. They're demanding, exacting, and averse to risk. They want confident vendors that bring more to the table than their products. Buyers need strategic partners that bring expertise they don't have to solve problems that are becoming ever more complex. Marketers have the knowledge to do so. They just need to match it with the skills required to create strategies and approaches that will result in successful execution tied to business objectives.

Creating content your audiences find useful has been the rallying cry for content marketing for at least the last five years. Quality content can be found in every medium and channel. It's no longer enough. Business-to-business (B2B) buyers crave meaning and connection—not just utility or value. That's a distinction that raises the bar for relevance and what marketers must achieve to create sustainable growth for their companies in the future.

Given the ease of publishing, marketers have gotten themselves into a bit of a pickle with buyers. They've published so much content without a strategy or the ability to speak to what matters to target markets that prospective buyers continue not to trust content produced by vendors. Buyers think vendor content is biased and lacking substantiation for the assertions it makes. Therefore they trust it less, just when we need for them to trust it more.

There is a silver lining. Buyers want to buy. They want to do so faster than they do now. They're also solving problems they've never had to solve before. Your buyers know they need help finding and deploying the right solutions. But they're stymied by the information they find online that doesn't address what they need. They're expending so much effort to make the right decision that it's taking longer, involving more stakeholders, and introducing risk that keeps them from making a choice. And the inconsistency they experience across channels isn't helping.

Marketers know relevance is critical, but they need to understand what it truly means in action and how to accomplish it. *Digital Relevance* will arm marketers with a comprehensive approach to learn the skills they need to correct these issues and iterate their way to being so damn relevant that their audiences can't help but engage with them for the expertise needed to solve their problems. With this competency, they'll help their companies reverse the credibility gap and help their buyers get on the fast track to problem resolution by creating better connections with depth of meaning. They'll be equipped to master the contributions that content marketing can make in any digital situation, with any stakeholders, be they customers, buyers, sales teams, industries, or the executive board.

As buyers and customers become more self-sufficient at researching solutions to their problems, marketers are shouldering more of the responsibility to make sure their companies build awareness, are viewed as credible, and display enough expertise to get invited into the purchasing conversation. *Digital Relevance* is your guide to ensuring that this happens.

PART 1

Strategy—Building the Foundation

Relevance and context must be understood as serving as the foundation for dynamic marketing in real-time environments. With sales cycles for complex sales often extending into years, maintaining relevance over the longer term requires strategic planning that's continually refreshed to account for market shifts and other developments. What's relevant today may not even catch your audience's attention next week or next month. This is true for prospects, customer retention, and the development of company advocates across the entire customer lifecycle, as well.

Given today's reality for marketers, the best way forward is iteration. Moving from a static approach to a dynamic one doesn't just happen. Becoming strategic is a mind-set that takes the big picture into account based on the impact marketing programs can make on business objectives. Achieving the highest level of relevance requires that marketers look beyond the campaign approach of one-off, unrelated interactions with buyers to a continuum approach that builds a story—positioning their companies as the perfect experts their buyers need to achieve their goals.

This first part of the book will provide the mind-set and strategic considerations that must accompany a successful transition to real-time, digital marketing that will result in radical relevance. The core components of strategy, including the relevance maturity matrix, personas, the continuum approach, and storytelling, will comprise the tools you'll need to ensure relevance across the buyer-to-customer-to-advocate lifecycle. By amplifying the distinct value your company provides in the eyes of your target audiences, marketing can be transformed from the creative department to a valuable corporate asset that has influence in aligning sales, product management, and customer service to deliver a consistent story that increases the value of the brand, no matter the type of interaction.

Each chapter will focus on the development of a skill or provide a tool that marketers will need to make the transition across the quadrants of relevance maturity. Depending on your level of maturity, some skills and tools will be immediately applicable. The rest will take work and effort to achieve over a longer term. The thing to do is get started and iterate as your competency improves. The payoffs in performance will provide the accountability your executive teams expect and position marketing as the growth engine of the company. Waiting is not an option.

SECTION 1

Relevance—The Frame for Engagement

According to the Chief Marketing Officer (CMO) Council, "B2B marketers invest an estimated $16.6 billion annually in digital content publishing to acquire business leads, influence customer specification and consideration, and educate and engage prospects."[1] The question to be answered is how well this money is being spent. Research conducted by Fournaise Group through its 2013 Global Marketing Effectiveness Program found that over 70 percent of marketers, "failed to deliver the (real and P&L-quantifiable) business results their Management expected them to deliver, i.e. more sales, more market share, more sales-ready prospects and/ or more conversions."[2]

The conclusion that Fournaise Group reached through interviews and the tracking of actual performance results was that marketers didn't spend enough time paying attention to the value their marketing programs conveyed. In other words, the relevance was lacking for their audiences.

Digital marketers are told to go forth and create relevant, compelling, amazing content and conversations. We've heard this so many times that it's become background noise. The problem with the instruction is that it's ambiguous, as well as subjective, which raises questions, including, What does it mean? How do I do it? What difference will it make? However, the ambiguity reaches further than this. The directive doesn't stipulate that marketers should take a continuum approach or that a strategy is necessary to produce continually high performance from digital marketing.

In many digital marketing departments, the team's conversation around content development goes something like this:

"We need a new white paper for a campaign next quarter."
"Why can't we do an infographic? Those are fun, and visual content is the big deal these days."
"What about a webinar? We can put one of our subject matter experts in the spotlight and generate leads at the same time.
The newest member of the marketing team at the end of the table, quiet up to this point, asks, "What are we trying to achieve?"
The other members of the team stop talking across each other and all eyes swing to him.
"What do you mean? We've got to produce 500 leads for the sales team next quarter." The Director of Marketing scans the faces of her team and sees doubt flicker across them. "We should do all three. That will help us make sure we reach our goal."
Heads nod, and the planning gets immediately underway to brainstorm the layouts for the campaigns, discuss the cool topics du jour, and define timelines for execution. The company's themes this year are focused on productivity, efficiency, and collaboration, so each of the three campaigns is assigned one of the themes.

I've been in many discussions similar to this one. Do you see what's missing? At no time during this meeting was there any discussion about the audience...the buyer. No goal, other than net-new lead generation, was considered. There was no discussion of how any of the three campaigns fit within a strategy, other than the mention of themes that this fictional company is approaching separately. When it comes time for distribution, the content will be published on the website, maybe additionally on an industry site as a paid placement, promoted via the company's social media profiles and perhaps by a third-party newsletter to that publisher's audience to source more new leads.

This doesn't necessarily mean that the content will be awful. It could be solid, researched, and well-written, high-level content. But the problem is in the altitude. Without a focus on the target audience, it will never come close enough to the ground to engage anyone beyond a cursory look. The content just won't be useful enough. The content will miss out on its potential to be considered valuable to any one role or persona because its orientation will be for a broader audience, rendering the information shared as shallow and wide, rather than deep and narrow. This approach results in content that is, if not irrelevant, at least much less than visionary.

You may be wondering why this matters. A survey of B2B buyers conducted by DemandGen Report found that 82 percent of senior executives said that content was a significant driver of their buying decisions. Sixty-one percent of buyers agreed that the winning vendor delivered a better mix of content appropriate for each stage of the purchasing process.[3] The significance of this last statement should not be dismissed. Right-time relevance is critical to ensuring that the information delivered to a prospect or customer is matched to the questions they are asking in relation to where they are in their buying process. Just because information will appeal to your buyer, doesn't mean that it will carry the weight you need it to whenever the decision is made to send it. As the adage goes, there's a time and a place for everything. It's now up to marketers to understand and act on what it means to match content with the context of buyer situations. The caveat to all of this is that relevance is difficult to establish and maintain without a strategy.

Context: The Cornerstone of Relevance

There's not a doubt in my mind that marketers know that everything they do—every program, email, content asset, social media post, and idea—needs to be relevant. The conflict is in what the term "relevance" means in application. From a marketing perspective, context is the set of facts, the meaning, or the circumstances that define a prospect's or a customer's intentions or needs in relation to an interaction or experience.

If a prospect arrives at the homepage of a company's website looking for thought leadership, and a pop-up displays asking them to sign up for a product demo, the interaction is out of context. Similarly, if an email promises information on a specific topic and the prospect clicks, landing on a web page that doesn't mention the idea that captured their attention and motivated their behavior, the experience has violated context. This last example is commonly referred to as "bait and switch." And it happens more often than it should.

A prospect who downloads a report about the latest trends in productivity, only to receive a call from a salesperson who wants to talk to them about buying productivity solutions, is also out of context. Context also applies to the expectations set by the content or messaging that motivates engagement—the promise made. In this example, the promise was a report on trends for productivity. The person downloading the report expected to gain access to that information. He did not expect that interest to indicate that his intention was to buy a productivity solution—at least not as a stand-alone action. The action taken by the salesperson is out of context and, as such, will likely be interpreted to be pushy, pitchy, and intrusive. It will leave a memory that can tarnish the experience the prospect had with your brand.

The next time you present a content offer, the prospect will remember the sales attempt rather than the quality of information they received in the report. Because memories are selective, people tend to remember high and low points of an experience more than the overall experience or the details due to the level of emotion attached to those low or high points.

Think about how the way you market has changed with accessibility to big data and your ability to reach out to individuals anywhere, anytime. Traditional marketing was one-to-all. Then the technology improved, and marketers separated marketing communications between prospects and customers. With further improvements, marketers have been able to segment their databases to message to smaller and smaller groups, or niches, of prospects and customers in an attempt to become more relevant. Now, there is technology in place to target even more closely based on a variety of factors. Iterations made by marketers who have embraced personas and customer-centric approaches have helped improve responsiveness and engagement. This is based on their ability to more closely match content and messaging to the context of their target audiences.

Context amplifies the relevance of digital marketing to create profitable engagement. The challenge is in how marketers can develop the skills and shifts to their mind-set that will improve the level of relevance they can achieve. As relevance maturity is reached, context will be addressed by extension. This is the framework for relevance.

The Relevance Maturity Matrix

In this section, you'll learn about the Relevance Maturity Matrix (RMM) and how a process for continuous improvement will enable your marketing team to tweak and refine strategy progressively to keep your brand relevant in the face of change. The RMM will help you understand the levels of transition and what it takes to move from one level to the next, as well as what can cause you to slide back. The skills and tools provided throughout the chapters will prepare you to become more dynamic and responsive than you've ever thought possible and develop the ability to continue to adapt amid continuous change.

There are four quadrants in the RMM: irrelevance, shifting relevance, social relevance, and radical relevance (see Figure S1.1). It is quite possible—as well as likely—that enterprises with a number of marketing departments and the sales team can each be in different quadrants of the matrix at the same time.

The RMM will be most effective if used as the standard to evaluate relevance across channels and the company to establish processes for continuous improvement specific to each area in relation to the quadrant it occupies on the matrix.

The least effective quadrants of the RMM are Irrelevance and Shifting Relevance. These two quadrants are based on an inside-out approach that puts the company and its products first. Most companies have departments that continue to function in these areas, if not all departments, perhaps making occasional forays into social relevance, but are unable to sustain the transition due to the lack of skills and mind-set required. An example could be a report created to speak to challenges faced by a target audience and shared with that target audience, while at the same time sending out product-focused promotions to the entire database. The company's relevance increases with the report, but this relevance quickly regresses with the continued product focus in its communications.

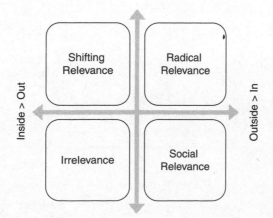

Figure S1.1 Relevance Maturity Matrix.

Social Relevance is being achieved by some companies as they work to embrace an outside-in approach, putting their focus on customers first, at least in application to customer-facing interactions in social channels. Radical Relevance is the quadrant of mastery that we should aspire to achieve. Becoming radically relevant is happens when marketing, customer service, and sales have adopted the outside-in approach with commitment that matches capabilities. It is important to note that, as in all things, mastery is not once and done. It takes continual effort to stay at the top level of any skill

The purpose of the RMM is to help digital marketers develop a culture of customer obsession that results in the level of relevance necessary to earn and sustain a competitive advantage in the markets their company serves.

Wouldn't it be wonderful if marketers could flip a switch and have their communications become so relevant that, when they talked, they commanded the same interest that a new product launch at Apple attracts? This book will help digital marketers become relevant to their audience and build this type of credibility in their communities. Although flipping the switch may take longer than you'd like. Achieving relevance takes work, commitment, and elbow grease, and works best when approached as an iterative process. The reality of continuous change means that even if you reach mastery today, you'll have to stay on your toes to keep it. That's exactly what *Digital Relevance* prepares you to do.

CHAPTER 1

Irrelevance

Being irrelevant is being beside the point, immaterial, unconnected, unrelated, or inapplicable to what your prospects or customers care about. Irrelevance happens when companies are self-focused, when they care more about what they want, need, or think than what their customers want, need, or think. Scenarios of irrelevance play out every day, with some of the most common including:

- A prospect fills out a form to download a white paper and is sent to the sales team as a lead. One survey found that 50 percent of marketers are routing the "leads" they receive directly to sales for follow-up.[1] One form completion does not a lead make.
- Emails arrive in prospect inboxes that the prospects never opted in to receive. Sixty-three percent of B2B marketing states that they are buying early-stage leads.[2]
- Nurturing programs are simply "drip" campaigns designed to deliver some type of content at regular intervals with the sole intention of keeping the company name and logo top of mind.
- Digital newsletters are focused on company achievements, new products, new staff hires, awards, promotional offers, and other inside-out content, without much thought about what will engage customers—or without understanding that the content is irrelevant.
- Facebook pages include silly contests, sports team updates, humorous photos, and company event pictures with which employees and people who will never become the company's customers engage.

- The corporate Twitter profile is a string of posts that includes the titles and links to company blog posts and promotional offers, repeated over and over again. There is no attempt to curate anything of interest or to become a resource for information that is not company produced.
- LinkedIn discussion group participation consists of posting the title and URL to a blog post with the first few sentences of the post as the "discussion topic." There is no conversation established and no follow-up to any comments that may be contributed by group members who are left alone to "talk" among themselves.
- The most updated area of the company website is the press release section where announcements about new customers, new talent acquisition, and new product launches or updates are the norm.
- Webinars the company holds are product demos.

I could go on, but you get the idea. How many of the above ring true for your company? These examples are traditional marketing masquerading—and not very well—as content marketing. It's sometimes hard to blame marketers, as many of them are doing what they've been trained to do or even, unfortunately, what they're allowed to do.

A survey of 1,000 US marketers asked them about their biggest concerns with digital marketing. The report found that things are shifting even more quickly than marketers thought and that their ability to keep up is declining rather than improving.[3]

Some of the findings from the report include the following:

- Seventy-six percent of marketers think marketing has changed more in the past 2 years than the past 50 years.
- Only 40 percent think their company's marketing is effective.
- Sixty-eight percent feel more pressure to show return on investment (ROI) on marketing spend.
- Most marketers don't have any formal training: 82 percent learn on the job.

While there are many areas of shaky confidence in relation to digital marketing, the top two concerns for these marketers were their ability to reach customers and their ability to keep up. And the kicker? Only 9 percent of these marketers strongly agreed with the statement "*I know our digital marketing is working.*"

Given all of this feedback, the most surprising finding is that, even with mounting pressure for improved performance from marketing teams, dedicated training has not yet become a priority. How can companies hope to address these changes and become more relevant to their prospects and customers if they do nothing to contribute to evolving the skills of their marketing teams?

Skills Needed to Kick Irrelevance to the Curb

While the skills marketers need to compete are many, overcoming irrelevance must begin with the gathering and understanding of a depth of knowledge about prospects and customers. In addition to the ability to develop comprehensive personas, the skills needed to kick irrelevance to the curb in digital marketing and move up the maturity matrix include those described next.

Listening. The idea of "listening" came about when social media platforms became marketing opportunities. However, listening is not solely an external exercise. It should also be applied internally through the available data.

Every response from a prospect or customer is a listening opportunity, whether it involves viewing a web page, opening and responding to an email, clicking on a search result or display ad, or posting on a social network. In digital marketing, we must rely on the metrics from the online behavior of our prospects and customers, as well as the overall outcomes that contribute to revenue growth, to guide our digital strategy. Once marketers begin listening and develop a curiosity about what the online behavior and activities of their prospects indicate, they'll begin to become fascinated with how to further engage them. This is when the shift away from irrelevance can begin.

Multichannel Comprehension. Marketers must understand which channels are relevant to target audiences and which will provide them with the most benefit based on their marketing strategy and goals. Marketers are using a multitude of digital channels, including in-house email marketing, search engine optimization, social media platforms, pay-per-click and display advertising, third-party email marketing, webinars, blogs, websites, and more to reach their audiences.

What's missing for many is how to take an integrated approach to having the channels in use work together to create consistent and compelling experiences that will contribute to achieving the goals of their digital strategy. This ultimately means that it's necessary to make the hard choice not to adopt every new, shiny platform or tool that becomes available. Rather, marketers must choose strategically among the options based on where their audience spends time and how well able they are to reach them in specific environments. It's better to use one platform or channel very well than to use many of them poorly.

Pronoun Shifts. Making a move away from irrelevance will come easier if marketers can make the pronoun shift. Moving from "we" and "our" to "you" and "yours" will have the effect of making us stop and think about what we're saying. Oftentimes it's a matter of what we're comfortable with. Marketers know the products their company sells. They know the company they work for intimately, and they're proud of working there, as they should be. This makes it really easy to publish the company line. But when the audience doesn't engage, then marketers must learn to flip their focus. Very few of us work for brands that command instant attention, such as Apple, IBM, or FedEx, in their respective markets. Therefore, we need to work harder and be more conscious of how we construct our messages and conversations based on who is on the receiving end.

Product Replacement. Marketers need to create the language for talking about what their products enable their prospects and customers to achieve rather than about the features and functionality. For example, the company line might be all about the multitenant, cloud-enabled, CRM system with open APIs and mobile collaboration. Instead of that boring mouthful that means nothing to a sales executive, marketers should talk about what these terms mean for their intended audience. They should create a story about how their sales team will gain the ability to work from wherever they are with access to the latest information about prospects and customers and to ask and answer questions with their peers, which will help them collectively sell faster and better, for example.

Irrelevance in Action

One of the first places to look for irrelevance is on the corporate website. Start with your about page. Will you find the phrase "[company name] is the leading provider of..."? My guess is that, if not those exact words, you'll find something close. When evaluating the way your company talks about itself, take a careful look at where the emphasis is placed: on your company or on your customers. Even a few misplaced words can skew the meaning.

Some examples to consider:

- "We are committed to providing a level of service to our customers that *makes us a leader in the industry.*" Notice how this sentence conveys that the company is more concerned with being seen as a leader than in serving its customers.
- "*Our company has shaped the future* of business by creating unprecedented value and opportunity for our customers." This sentence is reminding customers that they couldn't have found success without the company. A bit presumptuous and self-focused, to say the least.
- "*We are focused first and foremost on creating long-lasting customer partnerships by collaborating with them to identify their needs and provide solutions that support their success.*" Notice in this sentence how customers are front and center. If "their" was replaced with "your," it would be even better.

The intention of each of these sentences was probably to focus on customers. However, the placement of emphasis and just a couple of words shifted the focus back on the company for two of the three examples. Irrelevance can be sneaky. It's up to marketers to commit to the vigilance necessary to move past it by paying more than lip service to the concept of relevance.

Overcoming irrelevance is often a struggle due to marketers' ingrained habits in regard to communicating about their products and solutions. One of the biggest challenges is to figure out how to overcome the curse of knowledge. You simply know too much. You understand the functionality and the value and therefore make jumps in assumption that can leave your prospects scratching their heads in confusion or deleting your message with annoyance. As you develop curiosity from listening, gain the ability to evaluate channels objectively, and recognize inside-out language, you'll begin to see opportunities to shift toward the next quadrant of relevance maturity. Each time you create content and programs, stop and ask what makes them about the customer and why they should care. Taking the time to answer the question "so what?" will help you make the shift.

CHAPTER 2

Shifting Relevance

Relevance is a tricky construct. It's not something you can buy and own. Relevance is a skill that must be developed and honed both over time and in response to real-time shifts in the market. Being relevant is a new habit that must be developed and committed to. As marketers work toward helping their companies become a more trusted and credible resource in an environment in which buyers have control, it's easy for vigilance to slip and shift back and forth from inside-out to outside-in with their messaging.

During the presentation of a webinar about creating contagious content for a corporate client, one of the questions I was asked was how to handle the following situation:

The boss of a marketer in a life sciences company came to him with a request for an article for an online industry portal, with the main focus on a complex laboratory testing tool, complete with which functionality to emphasize and the three points about the features to include. The marketer knew that what the boss was requesting was "off" message for the personas that comprise the audience that interacts on the portal. The deadline for the article was the next day. There wasn't time for negotiation or building the case about why the marketer wanted to approach the assignment differently. So what should he do? How could he create something relevant given the parameters he had to work with?

I'm pretty sure we've all experienced this dilemma in our work as marketers. I'm also pretty sure that these types of requests won't fully disappear for some time to come. The recommendation I gave was to do just what the boss asked, but to focus the messaging on what the audience would care about. When writing about a product feature, put the emphasis on what it will enable the prospect to achieve, rather than the technical details that might be the obvious choice, as seen, for example, in the functionality and points that the boss wanted covered.

Conveying value with words is one of the most important responsibilities for marketers of complex products. When confronted with a situation, such as in the example above, we can revert to product and company "speak," or we can take a customer-relevant approach to the assignment. By assessing his boss' request from the perspective of how he could make the three points in a way that would be to his audience, the marketer was able to overcome the standard response that would have probably produced content that ended up as "shelf ware" on the portal, or even worse, portrayed his company as irrelevant. Validating this probability, the B2B analyst firm Sirius Decisions presented research at its summit in 2013 that stated, "60 to 70 percent of content churned out by b-to-b marketing departments today sits unused."[1]

There are many reasons why content goes unused, including lack of search engine optimization, and lack of distribution and promotion, but the biggest reason by far is that it's simply not relevant and doesn't match the audience's context. In an online poll conducted in January 2014, when marketers were asked what they thought the primary reason was for content going unused, the top response was that the topic is irrelevant.[2] Therefore, it follows that if nearly 70 percent of content goes unused, then only 30 to 40 percent of the content that marketers produce is relevant. This also means that 70 percent of the budget spent on content development is wasted. One reason for this could be that marketers, in an attempt to become more relevant, take a neutral stance.

Neutral Is Not a Strategy

Neutral is middle of the road. Neutral means not putting a stake in the ground. Neutral is indefinite. But, worst of all, neutral is boring, and it says your company doesn't care. When buyers look to your company for input, advice, expertise, and thought leadership, a neutral position is disappointing and makes your company infinitely forgettable. Buyers have a lot to learn when trying to decide whether or not to solve a problem or even if it's worth their time, effort, and money to take any action to change at all. Neutrality doesn't help them gain confidence. They can't use "neutral" to justify or inform a decision.

A neutral stance could be a blog post written about the pros and cons of moving to the cloud, for example. The pros and cons are equally rated with five points for each side. The company that authored the post never takes a stand on whether one side outweighs the other. Therefore, the reader has no idea how to relate to the company because it has remained neutral. Even if one of the pros or cons resonates, the viewer will take away the information, but is not likely to relate it to your company after the fact.

It's even worse to take a neutral stance in established relationships. Your customers are bound to lose faith in your company's capability as a partner if your message is neutral. They are continuously looking for sources of competitive advantage in their relationships with vendors, and they're not going to find it if your position in the marketplace resembles the stance of Switzerland.

The reason that marketers choose a neutral stance is because they're not confident enough in either their knowledge of the audience or that their company will support the change to a customer-centric focus...or both. The perception is often that neutral is better than being totally focused inside-out. Neutral can be seen as an improvement that will also protect marketers' jobs. Not stirring the waters is a common approach when a company's culture isn't friendly to change. But the very idea of sitting on the fence makes it easy to fall back to a reliance on messages about company and product. It also makes it easier to fall forward to a more customer-centric approach, but the perception of risk is still high enough to keep that from happening too often.

Marketers must be bold enough to gain the skills, shift their mind-sets, and learn the next practices that will help them get beyond a shifting mentality for relevance. Otherwise, their companies will go unnoticed by buyers who need the ideas and insights that can help them achieve their goals. Looking elsewhere is only a click away.

Skills to Vanquish Shifting Relevance

It takes commitment for marketers to avoid falling back into irrelevance. Even more than that, it takes perseverance and a bit of a bold approach. To vanquish shifting relevance, marketers must begin to put strategy ahead of tactics. This includes the ability to become a ruthless editor, see the big picture, and switch from a focus on transactions to a focus on relationships.

Ruthless Editing. There's a phrase you learn as a writer: *the courage to kill your darlings.* This means having the ability to delete the words that don't work by looking at them with a realistic eye that has no room for the thin-skinned emotion of authorial attachment. If you're editing someone else's work, do this kindly, but the focus must remain on the audience, or else the content developed for your digital marketing programs will be sentenced to purgatory and sit unused.

Reading content out loud is one of the best ways I know to ensure that you really "hear" what's being said. You'll find out whether your sentence structure is unwieldy, and you'll learn whether you're connecting the dots from sentence to sentence and paragraph to paragraph. It is best if you've developed a premise for each content asset, as well as goals that help you remain biased toward your customer when editing for clarity and purpose. By approaching your content with a relentless intention to deliver something your audience will find valuable, the chances that your audience will agree improve dramatically.

Ruthless editing can also be helpful when applied to our thinking as marketers. To make the transition, we must become adept at recognizing when we are slipping back toward irrelevance and take corrective action.

Big-Picture Perspective. Traditional marketing was based on short-term campaigns and quarterly themes. Unfortunately, these constructs still exist for some companies. As the tide of control has shifted squarely to buyers, and complex buying cycles can run many months—or even years—marketers need to gain the skills to take both a short- and long-term view. Obviously short-term goals must be met to support sales goals and serve as a barometer for performance, but the long-term view across the entirety of the customer lifecycle is required for sustainable strategy and quantifiable contribution to revenues and company growth. Marketers must start to adopt a continuum approach.

Digital marketing is not a one-shot deal. Buyers are using content to learn what they need to know to inform decisions. Marketers must look at all of the interactions necessary to make this conversion happen. Focusing on only one interaction at a time makes it easier to fall back into irrelevance. Putting the big-picture perspective to work requires a strategy, a plan. With a plan, it is more difficult to regress because it's a violation of the forward momentum that is designed into the long-term approach.

Building Relationships. There is a difference between the simple, one-off transactions prevalent in traditional marketing and creating useful and valuable interactions that build business relationships based on the recognition of mutual value that can result from digital marketing. In a complex B2B purchasing environment, not only must marketers build relationships between individuals and their company, but they must also help those individuals convince others to collectively reach consensus about the buying decision.

Digital marketing is not best served by building a relationship with only one contact at a prospective company. Marketers must determine all the players involved in making the decision and attempt to engage as many of them as possible, given the resources available. The reason for this is that buyers are self-educating. They are savvy about doing research and finding information that informs their choices. That most buyers don't engage with a salesperson until after their short list is created is well known. Savvy marketers know that building relationships that get their company's ideas in the room—even if their company isn't present—is the key to getting on those short lists and helping their salespeople gain entry into those critical buying conversations.

As marketers develop these skills related to how they view the objectives of digital marketing, they become more committed to the goal of achieving higher relevance. For relevance is truly the only way forward. This shifting back and forth from inside-out to outside-in messaging will become a relic of the past as marketers move to the next quadrant of maturity by embracing a social mind-set.

CHAPTER 3

Social Relevance

It's no secret that the channels available for digital marketing have exploded over the last few years. Evidence of just how much growth has occurred in this field is represented by the Marketing Technology Landscape Supergraphic that Scott Brinker from Chief Martec.com has been compiling since 2011. In that year, the marketing technology landscape included 100 companies; in 2012, it grew to 350; and in 2014, the number of companies includes nearly 950. There are 43 categories organized across six major classes.[1]

From a channel perspective, most marketers are confronting the reality that many of the new channels—if not based on social networking—certainly include an element of social. Even the corporate website often now includes the capability to share content and comment on the company blog, if not elsewhere. Social sharing options are also commonly included on email templates used for nurturing programs and demand generation. It's probably fairly accurate to say that—after email—most of a marketer's distribution strategy for published digital content is based on posting links to it from social platforms.

As marketers have made the transition to digital marketing and as buyers have become more exacting and demanding, the shift from push to pull marketing has been more successful in some cases than others. This is obvious from the number of posts on social media that are purely intended to be communications pushed or broadcast to audiences that are thought to be reachable through social platforms. However, this approach relegates marketers to irrelevance or, at best, shifting relevance in the RMM.

Social relevance is based on conversational competency. Rather than a broadcast approach that is based on traditional "push" methods, social relevance is about context and idea expression. Conversational competence is the difference between posting a title with the link to a blog post without any additional context versus posting a relevant reason for your audience to read the post with a link to it, for example.

Think about the components that comprise a conversation. For example:

Heading back to his office from the break room, Dave sees his colleague, George, walking down the hall.

"Hi, George. Have you seen the latest report on email engagement?"

George finishes texting and slips his smartphone into his pocket before looking up. "Hey, Dave. I just got it today. I haven't had time to look yet. Did you find anything interesting?"

"Yeah, I did. At one point, the analyst is talking about the need to shift from isolated transactions to interactive buying journeys. It really hit home for me why short-term campaigns are no longer as effective as they used to be. That's showing up in our metrics, too, right?"

"Unfortunately, yes." George raises his glasses and rubs the bridge of his nose. "We're seeing response fall off each quarter when we change themes. By the time we regain momentum, it's time to change themes again."

Dave nods. "It's like two steps forward and five steps back. The framework the analyst suggests for nurturing is based on longer-term storytelling methods. Do you think we can introduce this concept at the planning meeting on Friday?"

"I think that's a great idea, Dave. But we'll have to get Sally to buy into it. And it's going to mean a shift to our current agenda. Do you have ideas for how we can get her to cross over from the dark side?"

What do you notice in the thread of this conversation? A conversation is actually built on a series of questions and answers. It's a back-and-forth exchange that connects the dots throughout the thread of the discussion. A conversation creates a more fluid experience for both parties based on increasing the relevance with each exchange. When applied to a marketing context, the question-and-answer format of the "conversation" can be conducted over the duration of the buying process. Once the prospect becomes a customer, the conversation shifts, but it still continues. The tricky part of creating a conversationally driven thread that engages your audience is in integrating the channels in use to create a consistent and progressive experience over time.

According to research conducted by McKinsey & Company, "56% of all customer interactions happen during a multi-event, multi-channel journey," and "38% of all customer journeys involve more than one channel of interaction."[2] While this research focuses on a customer experience, rather than a prospect experience, the IDG Customer Engagement Study found that an average of eight informational assets are used to aid decision-making during the purchase process, accessed as the prospect completes each stage.[3] These findings help make the case for the integration of touchpoints and the need to eliminate the one-off, one-way mentality of traditional marketing approaches. Digital channels with easy access make connecting the dots for your buyers even more important.

Marketers need to understand that social relevance isn't just for social media applications. Whether within a single channel or across a number of them, social relevance is about connecting the story and ensuring consistency of experience, even as context shifts. For example, it is possible to create a dialogue successfully on websites by guiding visitors from one content resource to the next based on a topical thread or a problem-to-solution path. A lead nurturing program constructed as a serial "story" can also establish an ongoing dialogue, with each touchpoint added over time. And, yes, exchanges on social media can add depth and richness to the content shared to help build engagement and relationships if addressed as dialogue, rather than broadcasts.

Imagine that you receive a nurturing email from a company whose expertise you respect. You click to read the article the email directed you to on the company's website and then you see a link to a blog post. You click the link to the blog post, enjoy that it extends the topic in the article, and see that the company is hosting a webinar on the subject. You click to register, and it's immediately clear that the topic you're interested in is represented. You learn an additional fact in the bullets included in the abstract about the webinar that you had a question about. This added insight convinces you to register to attend.

In the above example, your experience was fluid, easy to follow, and increasingly relevant. Each step made sense, given where you were the step before. This scenario is an example of "conversational competence." While it may sound simple, the reality is that in many companies, three different teams would work on this content. What are the chances that the experience will even be connected, let alone conversationally competent?

The best way to accomplish social relevance is with an iterative approach. In other words, don't boil the ocean all at once. The complexity of digital marketing is high enough without your trying to do too much at once. Focus on becoming conversationally competent with one audience across channels and learn what works and what doesn't. Refine and tune your approach, and then add another audience.

Skills Needed to Turn One Way into Two Way

Social relevance is about two-way or even multidirectional experiences. At this stage in relevance maturity, marketers will be best served by thinking about messaging, content, and communications as a dialogue, rather than only considering what the "conversation" looks like from their side. Developing conversational competence will enable marketers to feed the dialogue, but they also need to consider who else in the company is initiating dialogues. In today's workforce, this is likely to include nearly everyone at the company.

Start by connecting the marketing silos. I've worked with companies in which the demand or lead generation team didn't speak to the social media team, and neither of those teams interacted regularly with the corporate communications team, for example. This is also the point of no return, which means that if you haven't done so already, consideration should be given to the establishment of a process for continuous improvement.

Additionally, with the intent to connect channels comes the need for technology that enables processes to be put in place, as well as real-time visibility into how digital dialogues are developing, or to learn why they're not. Some companies have implemented social listening technology, marketing automation technology, and heavy-duty analytics. But in many of the projects I work on, my contact has to request data from the team with the technology that has it. To overcome this limitation of silos, still other companies are starting to consider implementing, or are in the process of building, Marketing Centers of Excellence. Think of these as centralized teams that manage the content and conversational competence of the brand in order to pull together all the silos of skills and the technology that enables them.

Conversational Competence. Developing conversational competence is as much a mind-set as it is a skill. It requires determining how you want to represent your brand online, often in real-time circumstances, such as on social platforms. The tone, voice, and style used should also translate to your web properties, marketing content, and email messaging. Your efforts in one channel should not clash dramatically with your efforts in another, resulting in a Dr. Jekyll and Mr. Hyde experience for your audience. Although you must acknowledge that there are nuances in play for each channel, the content and messaging produced in one should reflect well in another because the probability that your prospects and customers will experience your messaging in more than one channel are pretty much guaranteed.

To get started with a conversational approach, you need to keep in mind how your audience will receive your message and what response it may generate. Just as in a face-to-face conversation where your response would be fluid, it should appear this way in digital expression. I know this sounds complex, and it can be, but consider a few options that can get you started simply and also result in the creation of an effective dialogue:

- The way you approach "see also" within your website content. Companies will often link to any word or phrase on a web page that allows them to direct their audience to a product or solution page. Instead, think about what the next best content offer should be based on the main topic or purpose of the page.
- Titles of blog posts are often written for search engine optimization (SEO) value. If you're going to Tweet about a blog post, what's the most interesting phrase on the page that is geared to what your intended audience cares about? Think context and use that phrase with a link. If someone replies or shares your post, what's a "see also" message you can reply with to try and extend their engagement and the dialogue?
- Discussions need more than a title and a link to content. One of the most misused social platforms is LinkedIn Groups. Consider the context of the group and present a premise for the content, followed by a question that provokes response. Make it useful and then be sure to respond when group members comment.
- Email messages are usually so much blah, blah, and blah. Try the conversational structure of question and answer based on the context of a specific audience segment or persona. Ask the question that your content answers, say why it should matter to them, and give them the link to get the answer. Your response rates should increase if you know the questions your audience must answer to consider buying what you sell.

These are only a few simple examples, but each of them requires the thought process that will help you achieve conversational competency. Building the rhythm of the back and forth that establishes a dialogue is half the battle. Creating contagious content that keeps the dialogue going is the other half, which we'll discuss as we go.

Connect the Silos. Marketing has somehow become a sprawling set of teams within many companies that work independently. It's not a surprise that brand tone, voice, and style differ across channels as they do across the organization. When one department has no insight into what another department is doing, it's a bit ridiculous to think they could all be in sync. This needs to change, and it needs to change at this stage, if not before. If a collaborative approach is not embraced across marketing disciplines, it is highly unlikely that your organization will ever reach radical relevance.

However, it is also ridiculous to think that this can be accomplished quickly. Start from where you are and work outward as best you can. For example, if you're responsible for the marketing programs for an industry vertical or a product category, map out what else touches your prospects and customers. What other teams have programs or activities that can "touch" this audience? A simple start is to establish monthly or quarterly meetings with those teams to gain visibility to what they're doing and show them what you're doing. Look for ways to collaborate and work together to gain traction and align the stories that are being shared. In some cases, you may even find that your efforts are duplicating someone else's, only perhaps not in an aligned sense. Collaboration can reduce this duplication and result in a higher level of social relevance that your audience will appreciate.

Continuous Improvement. As you are able to connect the silos and coordinate with other marketing teams, document new processes that result from improved alignment based on addressing audience context. Everything you learn about what works and what doesn't should be shared and documented so that improvements help inform the development of new programs and content focused on increasing response, engagement, and progression toward profitable relationships.

Prospects and customers also change over time. In one client's nurturing program, after about 18 months, we discovered that one persona was no longer as involved in the buying process as they had been. What the data showed was that there was an entirely new role that needed to be addressed. In this case, the change was due to the growth in the application of data being used in the area of the company to which my client sells. Had we not been monitoring this change and updating our insights from the sales team, our marketing programs could have fallen back into a lower quadrant of maturity. Instead, we were able to phase out one persona and introduce a new one to maintain a balanced approach to buying committee engagement.

There's much to be said about change management and developing processes for continuous improvement. To keep it simple, the point is that systematizing workflows and refining objectives based on improved visibility needs to be acknowledged as the key to keeping the forward momentum going. Changes that will improve your relevance maturity will have less chance of gaining commitment when an ad hoc approach is taken.

Technology Enablement. As mentioned at the beginning of this chapter, marketing technology is now available for pretty much everything a digital marketer needs to do. From automating nurturing to listening on social media to understanding the dwell time on a page or identifying patterns of behavior across the buying process or customer lifecycle, there's a tool, platform, or solution that can help. The biggest problem I see for digital marketers is that many have not learned how to use these tools to their advantage. Rather than adopting tools designed for business users, many companies have established teams to run the software for them. If these teams do not sit in marketing, the result is that the companies have simply relocated the information technology (IT) queue.

As marketers are designing digital programs to increase response and engagement, they also need to recognize that the more they are able to use the technology to advantage, the more responsive and engaged they and their teams can become. I remember a recent project in which a resource to which I needed access for a program was pulling an error page on the client's website. When I asked for it to be fixed, marketing had no option beyond asking the IT team. The response was that it wasn't a priority for IT. Another project required a two-week lead time to publish a blog post. This type of approach is hindering rather than helping marketers achieve success with digital marketing programs.

On another project that was focused on helping a new vertical that tended to be late adopters of technology improve the way they used data, the team was able to publish content in real time and gain access to data as programs were executed. With the visibility to see what was working and what was not, marketers were able to continuously refine their digital marketing programs.

The program contributed to five deals worth more than $15M in revenue in 18 months. Before the program began, the company had defined the buying process as taking, on average, three years to close a deal—due to the size, price, and complexity of the solution.

Digital marketing needs to run at the speed of your prospects and customers, not the speed of the IT department. Technology must be used to enable successful programs and insights as close to real time as possible. This doesn't mean that every marketer should become proficient at technology, although that wouldn't hurt. But it does mean we need to use technology to our benefit. There's a reason the role of digital technologist is gaining prominence.

Social relevance is about the rhythm of engagement. It's about developing the capacity and capability to anticipate and address the context of your audiences gracefully. All of the skills you've learned up to this point are foundational for moving to the mastery realm of the RMM, radical relevance. Without these shifts to skills and mind-sets, it will be infinitely more difficult to gain and keep the level of mastery that radical relevance requires. But with these skills as a foundation, not only are you ready but you are also armed and engagingly dangerous.

CHAPTER 4

Radical Relevance

Radical relevance occurs when marketers have reached the point of customer obsession along with the skills required to apply it strategically and maintain it tactically—even as prospects and customers continuously change. It is at this stage that digital marketing will reach its potential to drive sustainable and continuous business growth and influence the adoption of a relevance mind-set across the organization. Naturally, the bar is set high. But it is within reach.

Marketing has changed more in the last two years than in the last fifty. Buyers have also changed to the extent that 82 percent of CMO say their number-one concern is in their ability to reach customers.[1] The RMM is designed to enable digital marketers to turn these concerns into confidence backed by capability. As in the quadrants of lower maturity, there are a few more skills that will help marketers to sustain mastery of relevance.

Customer Obsession. Shifting your company to a customer-first approach is something every company should pursue. It's the level of customer centricity necessary to push boundaries. Customer obsession is based on deep knowledge, insights, and context that enable marketers to intuitively align the distinct value their company provides at the intersection of what their customers need. While technology may help companies execute on customer obsession, the strategy must precede the selection of tools and platforms.

Personas are foundational to customer obsession. But not just any persona will do. These will not be flat profiles that allow marketers to check the box on their to-do list, but will become active, in-depth tools that allow marketers to model digital experiences, refine them on the fly, and help their prospects and customers build the confidence to buy faster. When marketers become customer obsessed, they become naturally oriented toward aligning their messaging and programs with their buyers' context. Rather than thinking about how to promote products, they think first and foremost about how what their products provide, can enable their customers to find higher levels of success.

Scenario Modeling. Prospects and customers are demanding, exacting, and averse to risk. They want confident vendors that bring more to the table than their products. Buyers need strategic partners that bring expertise they don't have to solving problems that are becoming ever more complex. Customers need to continue to evolve from solving the problem that drove them to buy, to tackling new objectives and shifting marketplaces. The personas that will help digital marketers achieve customer obsession will also help them to model scenarios and design experiences based on providing what their audiences want, how they want it, and where and when they want it.

The reason scenario modeling is a mastery skill is because it's not just focused on a moment in time, but on the lifecycle of customer engagement. Scenarios must become experiences that thread together based on the continuous delivery of value, as perceived by the audience. These experiences must also address the multiple expressions of personas from buyer to customer to user, as well as how all of them interrelate. The level of complexity is high, but scenario modeling can help you make the transition from the concept of customer obsession to the expression of it with compelling experiences supported by content and conversations across channels. This skill is also what will enable marketers to approach digital marketing as a continuum, rather than a series of campaigns. The difference this will make to performance can be startling.

Predictive Analytics. With continuous change and the shift to digital behavior, marketers need not only to make the change from reactive to proactive in their marketing programs but also to be able to predict the probability of the outcomes desired. All of the technology we're using allows for the collection of a lot of data. However, data isn't the goal; rather, insights are. Marketers will develop the ability to answer questions they may not have ever conceived as possible to ask in the past. The answers will help them develop the ability to read and respond to patterns of behavior that indicate opportunities to make corrections or amplify what's working really well—not at the end of the month or the quarter, but in the moment.

Becoming predictive is akin to anticipating what's coming next, with a higher level of probability than gut instinct can provide. Most of the data marketers use today allows us to look backward to find out what happened. Hindsight may be twenty-twenty, but without the ability to ask and answer forward-looking questions of the data, our marketing content will be yesterday's news. But, more importantly, without key insights into buying behavior, the quality of the leads we produce will not be as high as it could be, and pipeline progression will stall. In fact, prospects who stall in the middle of the buying process is one of the problems I'm hearing the most about from the marketers and salespeople with whom I speak. Predictive analytics will help us discover more value from our nurturing processes as well as initiate more conversations for salespeople with prospects who have a higher intention of buying.

Relevance Maturity Is becoming a Marketing Mandate

Quality content can be found in every medium and channel. It's no longer enough to move the needle. B2B buyers crave meaning and connection—not just utility or value. This is a distinction that raises the bar for relevance and what marketers must achieve to create sustainable growth for their companies in the future. Consumers and business buyers have similar opinions about vendor content—that it's less trustworthy, biased, and not a significant influencer across the buying process. This narrowing of perspectives shouldn't be surprising as it's always been there. What's changed is our ability to see how it plays out and the data and research that can now be conducted far and wide by companies, as well as the customers they serve. Unfortunately, the opinion of both consumers and business buyers in regard to branded content is not high:

- "Similar to how consumers purchase a car today, 61 percent of B2B buyers report third party sites and feedback from business partners, industry peers or social channels as more important than conversations with a company's sales teams when making a purchase decision."[2]
- When asked to rate the impact of content types across the purchase process, consumers favored expert content, then user reviews, and finally branded content for affinity and familiarity. The only time branded content rated as high as second choice was during purchase consideration.[3]
- "buyers confirm that third-party research, analyst reports and trusted editorial coverage top the list of trusted sources, with just 9 percent thinking of vendors as trusted sources of content."[4]

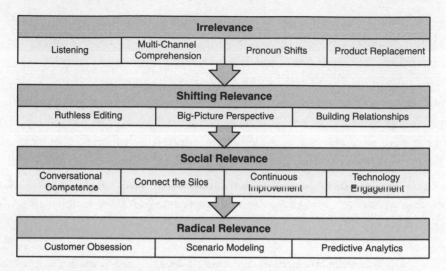

Figure 4.1 Skills for Relevance Maturity.

This is why ascending the quadrants of the RMM is key to developing and executing a digital strategy that drives results and revenues. There is definitely a silver lining for companies that embrace building the skills and shifting mind-sets to enable the achievement and sustainability of the highest levels of relevance: buyers want to buy, and they want to buy faster than they do today.

By approaching the RMM iteratively and learning the skills needed to develop an agile and radically relevant digital marketing practice within your company, you'll find that the performance goals set for the contribution to business growth will be achieved with a much lower risk of failure.

Positioning for Competitive Advantage

Brand positioning is becoming critical as more B2B marketers turn to content marketing across a range of digital channels to cultivate standoffish, self-service buyers. Your corporate positioning serves as the backbone for your content strategy. This is the framework that will hold it all together to ensure consistency and keep your story lines on track—no matter the channel in use.

The problem is that corporate positioning has traditionally been seen as a way to differentiate a company from its competition. However, brands look pretty much the same to buyers. Research conducted by the Corporate Executive Board found that 86 percent of buyers say they don't see differentiators between suppliers—and even when they do—it's not enough to warrant buying on value rather than price.[1] To gain competitive advantage in today's market environment, positioning must be designed around the intersection of your company's strengths and your customers' needs. This is representative of your company's distinct value. This is quite a different proposition, but one that can truly serve to help prospects become predisposed in your favor—as well as to instill confidence and loyalty with the customers that have already chosen to work with you.

Every company has a distinct value it provides that its customers need and want. If it didn't, it wouldn't be in business. Unfortunately, most companies see themselves as unique, but have difficulty articulating their distinct value. The result is that companies in the same industry make it difficult for customers to identify differences that matter. In a sea of "sameness," the industry leaders stand out from the rest, making them look like followers.

This sameness of approach becomes obvious when you look at the "about" statements for companies in a specific niche and each of them leads off with "[Our company] is the leading provider of…" type of posturing. How many "leaders" can there actually be in any niche? As with other buzzwords and jargon used by companies, this type of positioning becomes more blah, blah, blah that prospects ignore. It doesn't mean anything. Wouldn't you rather use this content real estate for words that set your company apart and resonate with your prospects and customers by communicating something more meaningful and relevant? Instead of trying to upstage their competitors by using the same words louder, companies must focus on connecting with customers.

For the purpose of a level-set for use of the term "positioning" in this book, I defined it as

> *The art of sharing your company's distinct value in ways that resonate with your buyers, compelling them to engage, trust, and—ultimately—buy from you.*

The point of positioning is to sum up the overall value your company provides that your customers will pay for. Get above the feeds-and-speeds minutiae. If you do this well, every approach and story you share will roll up under your positioning strategy. Your positioning will become the core thread that all of your marketing and communications carry to create consistency of experience for both buyers and customers. What you want is to know that even if your logo and company or product identification were removed from your content, your messaging would allow the audience to identify your brand.

The Role of Positioning in Spreading Your Story

As more channels entice new voices in your company to share about the work they do, the need to help them stay on track in aligning your brand story with whatever they choose to share is paramount. Providing them with a positioning story and guideline can be an invaluable resource for helping employees amplify the brand story.

But before this can happen, marketers need to clearly understand how and why different channels require different modes of communication.

- Twitter is about short bursts that spawn reactions, such as shares and mentions.

- Facebook thrives on personally related visual engagement that stirs response (likes and comments), and involves others (tagging).
- Blogs are a casual form of business expression, more textual in nature and focused on engagement through comments and social sharing.
- Discussion groups on LinkedIn are usually focused on aspects of doing business
- SlideShare works best when used as "flip books" to bring ideas to life, but goes even farther now with the ability to embed video and other formats
- YouTube is a distribution channel for video used by businesses to share customer experiences, expert interviews, and, often, to teach.

Even with the variances across channels, your company's messaging can be consistent and highly relevant across any channel in use, as long as the backbone—the distinct value—is represented. With publishing opportunities available to everyone, it's in a company's best interest to empower all employees to help spread your story far and wide. It's up to marketers to make sure the positioning resonates with them enough to be reflected in what they say and do. This doesn't necessarily mean the words chosen, but the flavor, the tone, and style, and the meaning behind the message. Positioning is often best when subtle. It's the consistency and intention that will shine through with relevant meaning.

Think about Joe in your software development bull pen who really wants to blog about the new features he's creating for customers. Or Linda, a subject matter expert, who has been invited to publish a thought leadership article on an industry news portal. What about Frank, in sales, who wants to get prospects into conversation faster and is participating in groups on LinkedIn? How about Karen, the VP of Business Development, who's giving a keynote speech at an industry conference? There are numerous opportunities available for everyone on staff to become a publisher. Ensuring they each have a clear understanding of the brand's distinct value is imperative for consistency of story and audience experience.

Give people the freedom to share their expertise in the context of a brand story built on what customers care about, without stifling their participation. Diversity in presentation can help improve the audience's perception of the authenticity and transparency of the company. As long as the underlying thread is always focused on the position you've established (are establishing) in the marketplace the consistency of experience will be perpetuated. After all, different prospects relate to different perspectives and styles. Positioning, used well, will serve to humanize your company by showcasing its subject-matter expertise with richness, depth, and context.

If it's not obvious by now, digitally communicating with prospects is no longer strictly a marketing role. As marketers carrying responsibility for the brand story, we need to facilitate how the brand is represented and positioned in the marketplace. It is paramount to remember that this story is not about products; instead it's about the distinct value products provide to your customers that they couldn't get from the vendor down the street.

Marketers must also gain the executive support needed to make sure that everyone in the company can articulate the value in relation to customer needs and objectives. How many employees at your company can do this today? Will their responses be consistent? Will those responses roll up under the positioning that's been defined for your company?

When your story is based on contextually relevant value and is consistently shared across all the channels where your prospects and customers will find it, marketers can help their companies orchestrate definitive competitive advantages by subtly guiding prospects to "get" how your brand differs from others they may consider. The reason why this is true is actually rather simple: it's because you've focused your brand position on your customers, not your competitors. This truly makes a dramatic difference to the level of relevance and credibility prospects and customers will assign to your company.

The chapters in this section will show marketers how to discern distinct value and create differentiation that their audiences care about; discuss what it takes to get an audience's attention by creating personas as active tools that drive strategy; and suggest how to align marketing plans with business objectives and how to develop engagement scenarios that result in unmatched customer experiences.

CHAPTER 5

Distinct Value Brings Differentiation

Regarding the value a company brings to its customers, the customer experience until the last few years has reflected what the company determined they wanted to present to the customer. The most dramatic shift that has left companies scrambling is the customer's taking control and dictating the experiences they want—sometimes, very vocally. With this change, customer expectations have become more demanding and less patient. Moving on is now the default response when relevance is lacking.

Because it's no longer up to us to decide what will make the customer experience special, starting with strategy is much more proactive than reacting to customer disappointment that the content we chose to share didn't meet expectations. Instead, marketers need to know what those expectations are and how what their companies provide can exceed them.

Distinct value is where a company's strengths intersect with what customers need. It is represented by the reasons why your customers really buy from your company. For this value to be distinct, it must reflect the outcomes your customers can achieve that they were unable to master prior to working with your company.

Distinct value is not the cool feature that you think everyone is clamoring for. Rather, it's whatever that cool feature enables them to do in a way that adds value to their own company. And it's likely that it's not about the "cool feature" at all, but an extension of the bigger value that your customers find represented by the whole solution, service, or product they've purchased. This is important to grasp because, as the key component of positioning, distinct

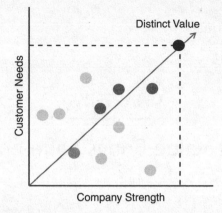

Figure 5.1 Distinct Value.

value must be reflected in all of your messaging and communications, across all the markets you serve and across all of the products you sell as a brand.

Distinct value fuels your brand identity, as recognized by the marketplace. This means it must also be reflective of your customers' perceptions and sentiments. Company positioning can be used to shift perceptions toward a new view in the case of a repositioning in the marketplace, which often occurs due to mergers and acquisitions or the turnaround or reinvention of a failing company. Your ability to reposition distinct value will be dependent upon consistency in the execution of compelling experiences tied to the new story.

Discerning Distinct Value

Distinct value is not about what your company does. It is about what your customers get.

A few examples of what companies are best known for include

- Volvo – safety,
- Google – find anything,
- Salesforce.com – no software (for sales productivity),
- Apple – smart design and compelling experiences.

Unfortunately, many businesses are hesitant to give up the company-focused messaging of the past for the customer-focused messaging that will bring advantages now and for the future. For example, on many "About" pages for corporate websites, you will find a statement that says something similar to "world's leading enterprise for X." But, elsewhere on the website, you may run into messaging such as "Simplify your business in ways you never thought possible" – from a business process company. Or "What would you do if you knew?" – from a data management company. This messaging is intriguing; it evokes curiosity to look further. It resonates. And, depending on who you are, it's infinitely more relevant than the copy on the company's "About" page. What is often a conundrum is why the statements that are relevant to customers are so different in context from the way a company chooses to describe itself.

Distinct value is not something best created in an internal vacuum. Assumptions are mutations of insight based on our beliefs and perspective. To truly discern your company's distinct value, you need to go to the source—your customers. When you interview customers, you'll want to ask both about their experiences buying, as well as using, what you sell. Don't take what they say first as the answer. Dive deeper to try and discover the emotional or professional (personal) criteria they used to determine value. And consider the role of the person and their level of involvement in the process. The best outcomes will occur when you can talk to a number of people involved, including decision-makers, influencers, and end users. After a number of interviews, you'll start to see patterns emerge. This is what you want.

One of the things I find the most interesting in many of the customer interviews I conduct for persona projects is that customers will often express some version of "they just seemed to 'get' us so much better than the other companies we considered." The reason wasn't price, company reputation, financial stability, superiority of functionality, or even references, although each of these points did play a role in some way. When it came right down to it, they wanted to work with the vendor that made them feel the most comfortable and best understood. I hear this feedback a lot. It's definitely worth considering how your company creates this "emotional" connection.

When you've completed all of your interviews, take all the responses to the questions about what each of the people you interview finds valuable and make a list down the left side of a page or whiteboard. On the right side of each, indicate why for each of them.

Function	Helen in Human Resources	Larry, Plant Shift Manager
Automation	Speed	Effort
Scheduling	Resilience	Speed
Skills Matching	Productivity	Risk

Figure 5.2 How Buyer Perceptions Differ.

For example, let's say a company provides labor scheduling software for the manufacturing industry. It is used by human resources to schedule workers and by plant managers to align the workers with the right skills to the right equipment to increase productivity on the line, resulting on higher output at lower cost.

Create a table that (in abbreviated form) looks like this Figure 5.2.

What you've learned in the interviews reflects different perspectives. Helen refers to speed as a value she personally receives from automation because the task is completed much faster. Larry, on the other hand, enjoys expending less effort. In relation to scheduling, Helen is responsible for ensuring the workforce doesn't suffer from fatigue that creates turnover. She's particularly focused on the tools of the solution that enable her to see time off and incidents that might reflect a need for a change in scheduling. In addition, she wants the ability to balance workers' hours to reduce the occurrence of fatigue, while maintaining the ability to meet demand. Larry finds speed to be the highest value here, as the system allows him to quickly match the assigned staff to the equipment that best suits them in the order he knows will keep the line moving fast.

When asked specifically what she liked about the skills matching feature, Helen responded that it helps her achieve better productivity levels—a KPI her performance is evaluated against. But, Larry says that the most important thing to him is the capability to apply the insights to skill sets to reduce the risk of injury on the line. He's evaluated on output from the line during his shift, and since human error is what causes injury or incidents that stop the line, reducing risk is the most valuable outcome from this solution for him.

The weighting by both Helen and Larry suggests that increasing productivity and lowering risk are the two key elements of value. Granted, that in a real-world scenario there would be much more data and input to analyze, this example is meant to give you an idea of how to discern your company's distinct value.

What you learn while doing this exercise may be different from where your messaging has focused previously. With automation, it's often assumed that speed and reduced effort are key benefits, but by looking at the value from the customers' perspective, you may learn something different, as we did with Helen and Larry.

To wrap up this example, a statement of distinct value for this company may look something like this: *Increase productivity on the line without increasing the risk of injury or incidents to ensure supply matches demand.*

This value statement has room in it to pivot to the other values identified for each role in order to enable the messaging and content created to cover all the ground it needs to. But with those two key values used as a thread in all of the communications designed by the company, relevance should remain high, while serving to continuously reinforce what's most important to prospects and customers.

Notice that the type of product is not included in the value statement. It is entirely focused on the most important outcomes that customers want and need. The software, in this case, is how they get it. The reason this is important is because it reminds us where to keep the focus. But it's not so tightly focused that it limits latitude in discussing other benefits or additional products that enhance this product for cross- and upsell, as long as we tie the story back to this distinct value.

The final step is to do a review of your competitors to make sure that the emphasis is distinct. The distinct value can be illustrated with explanatory messaging about how to apply and use it, but what you're going for is a value statement that is easy to remember and apply across the organization for the variety of people who will be publishing, sharing, or creating content.

While not optimal, I also know that many times divisions of larger companies must create their own distinct value based on the product category they represent or the to which industry they are responsible for selling. The main thing to remember is that the distinct value you find for the industry or the product group must also roll up under the broader corporate positioning. This way the divisional messaging remains in sync with the integrity of the brand.

CHAPTER 6

Personas: Distinct Value in Application

I'm a fervent believer that the foundation for relevance in marketing—digital or otherwise—is personas. I'm not talking about the flat one-dimensional one-sheets that skim the surface. I'm talking about the in-depth, comprehensive inquiry into the characteristics, attributes, and interests of the target segments who play a role in deciding whether or not to do business with you. The reason personas are needed is to put the focus of marketing where it needs to be—squarely on the customer. The better you know customers, the better this will work out.

Relevance isn't only about understanding your customers but also understanding their perspective on how what you sell enables them to reach higher levels of success based on their company's business objectives, as well as to enhance their careers. The only way to do this is for you to know them extremely well. The best way to maintain this level of knowledge and transform it into consistently relevant content and communications is to develop personas as working tools.

There are a variety of different flavors of external personas, from buyer personas to customer personas to user personas. Each one has a different context to be addressed. The personas for each company are unique—even if in the same industry—due to different business models, demographic and firmographic focuses, and distinct value.

- Buyer personas are focused on prospects looking to solve a problem or meet an objective that your products, solutions, or services help them to achieve. Buyer personas encompass all of the differing roles or stakeholders involved in the purchase decision and are usually represented by decision-maker, influencer, champion, and gatekeeper roles. Distinctions can also be made as to economic buyer and functional buyer.

- Customer personas have solved their initial problem by choosing your solution. This means their context must build from this new status quo to what's next. The objective for both customer and user personas is to create higher loyalty and retention, as well as increase account value through renewals, cross- and upsell. The roles represented by customer personas can include the person who "owns" the solution within the company, the executive(s) responsible for the department(s) its value impacts, and procurement or vendor relations.

- User personas are designed to address the perspectives of those who work with your products, solutions, or services on a daily basis. The goal is to help these "end users" achieve more complete use of the product and gain more value than they initially anticipated, as well as help them become champions for continued use, new additions, extensions, or feature upgrades.

Personas, therefore, cover the entire customer lifecycle. They are an active tool that can provide insights for strategies and decisions for the continuum of digital marketing programs designed to help the company achieve business objectives and drive sustainable business growth. The choices you make about how to increase your relevance for each persona will reflect your company's positioning and hinge on the distinct value identified.

The Components of Personas as Active Tools

Personas have been and remain a controversial topic for many marketers. Most commonly, personas are represented as one-sheets with a name and a picture. These simple constructs usually offer a few descriptive adjectives and high-level objectives, a demographic profile, and a short list of media preferences. Personas created with only this surface-level detail will not be of help to marketers as active tools, but rather serve as a checklist item that marketers can say they've completed. This is not their purpose, however, and is a waste of limited marketing resources.

Personas as active tools must be based on much more in-depth exploration that serves to guide engagement strategies for digital marketing and the achievement of higher relevance maturity.

For a level set, I define personas as:

A composite sketch of a segment of the audience represented by objectives they must achieve and problems they must solve based on the responsibilities of their role that align with what you sell.

I cannot emphasize enough how important it is to understand that a persona is not representative of a single, actual person. One of the biggest issues I see during persona creation is a response that skews the research by imposing a remembered encounter with a single customer onto a persona. I urge you to resist the temptation. Personas are not designed to validate your assumptions. One of the very interesting things about persona development is in gaining insights you did not already have and invalidating assumptions you find to be incorrect. Personas may not feel comfortable at first, but they will perform best if you allow the research and interviews to stand.

The personas I construct for client projects include the following.

First-Person Scenario

This is a "day in the life" written in the voice of the persona as if they are talking to you. These scenarios work out best if constructed as the final component of a persona, after all the research, interviews, and other components have been built. First-person scenarios should reflect the urgency, situational context, and level of intensity the persona has in relation to the problems they are trying to solve and the objectives they are trying to achieve.

This scenario should also include references to the other personas with which this persona interacts, for example, their boss or other executives who influence the line of business they serve, or their staff. It is important to remember that personas do not operate in a vacuum. Understanding their relationships with other stakeholders is especially important when considering the obstacles they face in taking next steps and how you will help them move forward to gain consensus.

Objectives, Obstacles, and Orientation

These three components constitute the core of the persona and will help you get a well-rounded view of the commonalities across the segment of focus.

Objectives are just what they sound like: goals the persona is trying to achieve. However, these cannot be high level, such as "increase revenues," but rather must dive deeper. For example, the equivalent of "increase revenues" for a contact center manager may be to increase the number of successful cross- and upsell offers her customer service agents make during a shift. In the case of adding depth to a high-level objective to "reduce costs" for the same persona, this may be represented by an intent to reduce average handle time for customer service calls. Objectives must represent the context of the persona as closely as possible.

Obstacles are whatever can get in the way of the persona's achieving their objectives. Depending on the role of the persona, these can be a failure of the persona to get buy-in from his boss, an incumbent vendor, loss of budget, perception of price higher than value promised, and more. The reason obstacles are important to highlight is that if marketers can address them earlier in the buying process, engagement can be sustained that might have otherwise been lost. Another result can be getting salespeople into the conversation faster, and thereby shortening time to revenue.

Orientation is related to the personal and professional details that are fairly common across this segment. Examples include being analytical, being prone to multitasking, enjoying mentoring staff, and being removed from day-to-day operations, to name a few. This area is very helpful for selecting the tone and style of the content you develop for this persona. For example, if your persona has an engineering background, they are more likely to have an analytical mind-set that orients them to engage with content based on statistics and supported with facts rather than with content based on suppositions and conjecture.

This area also includes education level and an average time in the position with the company or industry. One reason longevity is important is because it can be an indication of willingness to take risk. For example, an executive who's been with the company for ten years will know where the bodies are buried and will have built up a network of support. A lower-level manager with five or fewer years of experience may be a risk taker, but not have the network or clout to pull off gaining consensus for a transformational purchase.

Problems

The flip side of objectives is problems. If increasing successful offers for cross- and upsell is the objective, what's the problem that is keeping the persona from achieving it? Perhaps in our contact center manager's case, her agents are less successful because the number of screens they must navigate to find the appropriate offer takes too long, and the customer is already disengaging by the time they make the offer. Or it could be that the offers made are not relevant enough to the customer to whom they're speaking. Or, maybe it's that the agents' soft skills need some fine-tuning so they don't pitch too hard, turning the customer off.

Each objective has a corresponding problem. Looking at both sides of the coin, if you will, can provide insights that help you develop more well-rounded content that your prospects will find more valuable and relevant based on their context.

Questions

Based on the stages of the buying process your company uses and the persona's objectives, obstacles, and problems, define the questions this persona will have as they move through their buying process. The questions are nearly unlimited. You can add to them as you go, but I find it works best to start with a dozen, equally weighted across the stages of the buying process.

Based on the interviews and research conducted during the persona development process, brainstorm a list of questions your persona will need to have answered to gain the knowledge and confidence to keep moving forward with your company. Start by considering their status quo. What is the situation like today for the area you can impact? This is the equivalent of answering "why should I care?" in relation to the value your company provides. If you answer this question for the persona, what would they ask next?

Generating your slate of questions may not follow this linear path. Record all the questions that arise from brainstorming. You can always arrange the order later. Make sure also to think about how their need for information will change from stage to stage as you develop the questions.

Keywords and Phrases

For personas, this is not as much about search engine optimization as it is relevance and context. Given what you've learned about your persona, their objectives, problems, and questions, identify the long-tail phrases and keywords they will use to find information about addressing their needs. Do not include your company name or product names. You should be able to generate at least one short and one long phrase for each objective, problem, and question.

While getting your content found online is a critical factor for a digital marketing strategy, using the words your persona would use will help elevate the relevance they ascribe to your content because it will feel more familiar and be instantly more relatable. These keywords and phrases will also, hopefully, keep you from using industry buzzwords and jargon that hold less meaning for your persona.

Social Media and Online Destinations

This component of the persona is about discovering what these people commonly do online. Do they use social media? If so, which platforms do they use and how do they use them? Do they actively participate or lurk? Where do they turn for information that helps them do their jobs and which sites do they find credible? Do they attend webinars? Do they subscribe to industry newsletters? If so, which ones? Are there specific analysts that they trust or use more than others? Do they read blogs? If so, do they comment? Do they belong to industry communities? Are they responsive to email?

Answers to questions like these can help you determine where to invest your time and how to develop distribution plans and media budgets for digital marketing programs. Each persona you develop may respond differently based on level of role and the division of the company they work for, as well as the industry in which they work. Do not make the mistake of applying the insights for one persona across all personas.

Engagement Scenarios

Developing a persona is critical for gaining insights about a segment of your prospects, customers, or users, but marketers must also be able to get their attention and engage them in the channels they choose to use. Engagement scenarios are the equivalent of creating a simulated, interactive experience based on what you know about the persona to help determine your best course of action.

All personas will not engage across all channels, so it's very important to discern the differences among your personas based on orientation. Given what you've learned from your research and interviews, how would you go about attracting this persona? Where would you publish content to get their attention? Once you've gotten their attention, then what?

The point is to try to gain an understanding of what a plausible scenario might be so that you can make sure the content is connected in a way that presents the potential for the persona to continue their engagement with you. Engagement scenarios can be represented in editorial calendars and story-line design. They may also be added to, or adjusted over time, as you collect data about how the personas engage with your content.

Doing the Work for Persona Development

There are two key processes for persona development: interviews and external research. Start by interviewing your salespeople. Salespeople are involved in face-to-face conversations on a daily basis with potential customers. They are also nearly always happy to be involved and to share their perspective. It is also important to involve salespeople for a variety of reasons, not the least of which are

- getting buy-in for the personas that define the parameters for the leads and opportunities they will pursue;
- learning where prospects get stuck in the buying process so that marketing programs can be designed to help salespeople address those areas;
- learning why the company loses deals so that marketing can help address obstacles earlier in the process or as salespeople need ammunition to keep deals moving forward;
- gaining more insight to what happens to the leads you work so hard to generate and qualify for the sales team
- establishing a process for feedback from sales that will help you catch shifts in buying so that you can modify your programs accordingly.

When interviewing salespeople, I've found it best to interview them one at a time so that they provide their honest perspective, uninfluenced by others. Ask open-ended questions and guide the conversation, but don't provide input that may cause them to change what they'd say. In other words, don't lead the witness.

Next, you'll want to interview customers. It's best to interview recently acquired customers while the experience is still fresh in their minds. You'll want to talk to each of the buyer personas involved, if possible.

Create a list of questions that will help you gather information that will be helpful to filling out the components of buyer personas. You'll want to do enough interviews with both salespeople and customers so that you are able to identify commonalities. A sign that you've completed enough interviews is when you can identify a pattern of the same things being repeated. Those are the factors you'll want to isolate for each persona—the commonalities you're looking for. Remember that a persona is a composite sketch, not an actual person.

External Research

My favorite tool for external research is LinkedIn. Never before have marketers had access to so much personalized information about the types of people to whom they sell. Use advanced search to find profiles similar to the role and industry of your persona. Some profiles will be useless, but some of them will be virtual goldmines. Take note of how they describe their job and responsibilities, the interests they list, the groups to which they belong, and how long they've been in their roles. Pretty soon, you'll see patterns emerge that should mirror what you've learned in the interviews you've conducted. You'll also identify some additional commonalities.

Review analysts' research for their evaluation of the market the company serves and the competitors. Then visit any of the industry sites identified during the interviews you've conducted to understand what topics are being covered that relate to the objectives that have been identified for the persona.

Identify influencers for the persona and read their blogs or articles published on industry websites to learn what topics they're focused on. If comments are submitted, take note of what points people who are similar to your personas agree with, what questions they have, and whether those people are similar to the persona in development.

Finally, take a look at competitor websites, blogs, and social media profiles to see how their stories are presented. Do this last so that it doesn't influence your approach to the persona.

All of this information feeds the development of the persona. Refer back to the commonalities revealed by the interviews and match up what you've learned from the external research. Add in anything new that extends the information or helps add flavor and context beyond what you already have. As you finalize your personas, you'll realize that you've got an active tool—robust enough to create a ten-slide deck—not a flat one-sheet that doesn't help inform your digital marketing strategy.

It is critical to remember that personas change over time, just as buyers do. Make sure to update them regularly to ensure you have a perpetually active tool that adds value to your digital strategy.

The Value of a Persona

Creating personas with this level of depth that can be used as active tools contributes to achieving and sustaining relevance maturity. When creating digital strategy and execution plans for a considered purchase, marketers must be able to sustain the consistency of messaging and story line over a long period of time—ranging from months to years. Personas can help marketers better achieve their goals by

- enabling writers to grasp context and interests quickly to streamline content creation without veering away from the storyline;
- brainstorming new content ideas by determining all the different ways the persona's questions can be answered with content;
- optimizing resources by only distributing content in preferred channels;
- helping design the flow of a cohesive story across all buying stages to guide prospects progressively toward purchase;
- simplifying the effort to map content to buying stages;
- understanding how to revise or refresh existing content to get more return from investments already made;
- increasing company and brand credibility with target markets and customers;
- providing better ways to measure outcomes based on goals aligned with a persona's objectives.

CHAPTER 7

The Big-Picture Business Perspective

Digital marketing strategy is a means to an end—revenue. Everything on a marketer's agenda, including customer relationships, brand awareness, demand generation, and sales enablement, must contribute in some form to monetization. The success of each of these functions relies on how well you know your customers and target markets. IBM's CMO Insights Study, Stepping Up to the Challenge, states, "Enterprises with a deep understanding of their customers are 60% more likely to be financial outperformers."[1]

This study also found that 43 percent of the CMOs who are defined as Digital Pacesetters help their companies do better financially in comparison to 25 percent of Traditionalists. As defined by the study, Digital Pacesetters use data to become more relevant to their customers, are prepared for heavy social and mobile traffic across devices, and are actively integrating physical and digital sales with services channels. Traditionalists have barely begun to do these things.

For marketing to be seen as integral to the success of the company, the function must earn operational credibility. Digital marketing programs must connect to the metrics of business, such as contribution to revenue, customer retention and loyalty, and return on marketing investment (ROMI). Marketers also need to be able to communicate up the line about what they do and how what they do creates this impact. Crafting a story about clicks does not provide much of a story to tell that anyone will care about.

To make marketing meaningful to the organization, marketing must be driven by strategy that encompasses the big-picture business perspective, not one narrowly focused campaign at a time. While marketers need to move quickly to keep up, they would also be wise to slow down to do the foundational work that will result in sustainable and profitable speed. In the midst of change, embracing it productively requires understanding what's changing, why it's changing, what it means, and how best to address it given your position in the marketplace.

Change Kicks Campaigns to the Curb

Customers are no longer passively receiving information, but contributing their perspectives online and voicing their delight and dissatisfaction, along with making their expectations clear through their digital behavior. It's one thing to meet them online on their own terms. It takes a bit more effort to ensure that how you do so is strategically tied to achieving business objectives—theirs and yours.

Campaigns as a marketing construct are obsolete. The biggest reasons why campaigns are no longer working well is that they start and stop. Campaigns are like marketing in a box. Just when your prospects get interested in the story you're telling, the campaign ends, leaving them hanging. When you start a new campaign with a different topic or theme, you have to win them over again. Engagement isn't easy to gain. Why would you want to put it into question every month or two when you stop one campaign and start another?

Digital marketing, by its very nature, is an ongoing process of continuous engagement. Being perceived as relevant by your target markets is not something that works well in an on-off format. Relevance requires consistency. It is nearly impossible to achieve relevance maturity without a continuous and determined focus on our customers' needs, preferences, and expectations. If marketers allow relevance to slip, the result is a reenactment of the one step forward, two steps back idiom that results in retrograde performance. If uncorrected, each subsequent campaign can amplify irrelevance by proving that your company doesn't understand or care sufficiently about its customers.

The problem with campaigns is that the thinking behind them is narrow and that they are usually run in a stand-alone manner from other digital marketing programs. Campaigns are the equivalent of a "use-by" date on the food we eat. Short-term programs are a structure based on what companies want or need, rather than what customers want or need.

The quick-cycle nature of campaigns has trained marketers to get bored with the tale they're telling, so they think their prospects are also bored. The reality that prospects are just becoming curious by the time a campaign ends is more likely. But marketers move on to the next campaign with a new theme or topical approach. This creates confusion on the part of your prospects and leaves them wondering what the rest of the story was that they'd become interested in learning more about. Every time you change a campaign, your relevance ebbs. The introduction of a new theme requires that you reestablish relevance. The switch in topics and focus allows your prospects an opportunity to decide your content is no longer relevant to them.

Likewise, campaigns can leave your executive board wanting. Unless your "campaigns" run the length of the buying process, it's unlikely that they will provide the proof to validate that marketing programs are directly contributing to tangible business outcomes. Relevance maturity is not only a customer-focused initiative but also an organizational imperative. While the big-picture business perspective may seem to be beyond marketing's purview it is not.

This shift away from campaign mentality to a big-picture perspective is important because marketing carries a bigger load and has a broader horizon than it had just a few years ago when the responsibility for sharing the company's story was its primary domain. Now, the entire organization, your customers and your partners and suppliers can get in on sharing your story. In order to capitalize on the potential that has been made possible through online and digital tools, channels, and platforms, marketers must incorporate the bigger business perspective. Digital marketing today is similar to an act performing without a net. Because what's said about your brand by others is what defines it, relevance maturity that enables marketers to work competently with less direct control is essential. This type of influence in the marketplace will not be achieved with campaigns, but rather with a steady increase in engagement based on delivering consistent value that helps prospects find your brand steadfast and credible and that will become reflected in what they say about it.

This passage from a Forrester study, The Power of Customer Context, researched by Carlton Doty, VP, Group Director serving Customer Insights Professionals, sums up the power of today's buyers:

> *For all the activity you try to catalyze through campaigns, individuals more commonly interact with your brand outside of those campaigns. They may learn about your product or service prior to purchase. Then they'll use your product, connect with others and even organize activities around it. They spread word of mouth, positive and negative—and that, whether you like or not, is your actual brand image."*[2]

Big-Picture Thinking

As customers have wrested back control of the buying process and become more vocal and demanding, many areas of the company are experiencing new challenges, not the least of which are sales, customer service, and research and development. Marketers, as the facilitators of the customer lifecycle, can help each of these areas. Increasing relevance maturity is not just the mandate for marketing, but for the entire enterprise.

Here are a few examples of how digital marketing can become a respected value-add to the enterprise:

Sales. Salespeople are tasked to bring value and meaning that matters to conversations and digital exchanges with potential customers. Yet, buyers think they miss the mark more often than they hit it. Salespeople are encyclopedias about the products they sell, but often can't translate that knowledge into new ideas that will deliver strategic value to buyers, whereas buyers now know nearly as much about products as the salespeople do. What buyers want are new ideas, insights into where their industry is going, and creative strategies for solving problems and gaining competitive advantages.

While salespeople may know a lot about the products and solutions they sell, what's missing is context that can easily be translated into value. Given the data that marketing gathers about each prospect and account's engagement, this "small" data can dramatically change the way that salespeople prepare for and enter into conversations with prospects.

Imagine how much more meaningful a conversation a salesperson can have with your prospect if he knows at the handoff which content the prospect engaged with and the topics that indicate attention intensity, as well as links to content that will resonate perfectly as a follow-on given the prospect's recent behavior. While the activity of tracking web visits has been around for some time, the difference here is in the ability to add context based on engagement over time, not just a single visit to the website.

Customer Service. Just a few years ago, contact centers were cost centers put in place to resolve customer service issues. Today, they are becoming profit centers, with efforts being made to cross- and upsell customers based on intelligently matching offers to the customer's context. Customer service agents are also being tasked to interact with customers in a variety of channels, including social media, online chat, and email.

While customer service agents are trained to handle customer interactions related to product issues and billing inquiries, they are not necessarily equipped to "market" your company's products or to engage in these newer channels. Digital marketers have the experience, content, and insights to help to ensure that the conversations customer service agents hold with customers are relevant, compelling, and on point with the brand story.

Research and Development. R&D and product managers are under pressure to improve products and services, while continuously innovating to create competitive advantages that bring new customer acquisition, but that also retain and grow customer lifetime value. As relevance maturity is achieved, digital marketers will have the insights to supply R&D with insights that capture the nuances of how the customer is changing and what types of ideas and issues they're most responsive to. Digital marketers with higher relevance maturity can selectively "float" new ideas to stimulate dialogue and gauge market reaction prior to making the commitment to develop new features and functions. Their listening programs can provide insights progressively over time as market shifts occur.

One of the often overlooked opportunities in big-picture thinking is collaboration. While I've indicated some of the ways in which digital marketers can aid other departments, the reverse is also highly valuable. Sales, customer service, and R&D all have tremendous insights and data that can aid marketers in the development of better experiences and in making decisions about context in the development of digital strategies.

Big-picture thinking is about connecting the dots to share information cross-functionally to help the organization achieve business objectives. Marketers must learn to understand the financial ramifications their programs can have and which levers to pull to help the business achieve the best outcomes. Marketing must become about more than net-new lead generation.

The most valuable contribution digital marketers can make is in using customer insights to transform the performance of their own programs, as well as in translating this information into knowledge that, when shared cross-functionally, will help create tangible business impact. It's in this use of data and insights that marketers can contribute the most pervasively to the competitive advantages their companies wield.

CHAPTER 8

Customer Experience Brings Competitive Advantage

Customer experience is a top priority for digital marketers. However, most companies rate the concept higher in importance than they do the execution, given the lack of resources. As customers gain higher comfort levels with online interactions, a range of devices, and a variety of channels, they become hypersensitive to the experiences they have online—and they're not overjoyed. Meaningful Brands® research in 2013 found that "most people worldwide would not care if more than 73 percent of brands disappeared." This finding was based on 700 brands, over 134,000 consumers, and 23 countries, and measured the impact of 12 different areas of well-being to gauge the benefits of brands in relation to quality of life. The top brands outperform the market by 120 percent, and the top five are Google, Samsung, Microsoft, Nestle, and Sony.[1]

This consumer disconnect with brand touchpoints is caused by fragmentation, silos, and irrelevance and shifting relevance. The lack of caring by consumers is fueled by companies talking about what they want and continuing to deliver products based on traditional concepts of newer, faster, and bigger. As the research above indicates, this approach no longer resonates. What customers want is simplicity, consistency, and continuity in their experiences across brand communications that help them discover tangible value they identify with based on their needs, preferences, and expectations. In other words, they want relevance.

The end-to-end customer lifecycle is not the same as the one your strategy may be built upon. While executive roles may be held by people in their 40s and older, millennials—those aged 19 to 36—are over 76 million strong and have a completely different view of life than their bosses may hold. They look at life differently, and that's not likely to change, according to research by the Corporate Executice Board (CEB).[2] Where millennials embrace the idea of YOLO (you only live once), which drives their need for adventure and happiness, older generations embrace more traditional values such as integrity and justice, as well as the practicality of saving for retirement. From a marketing perspective, this presents a challenge in the nature of the experiences that will resonate with each. This is also true in complex B2B purchases when considering the influencers performing research and evaluation and the decision-makers with the budgetary authority. Even when marketing to a B2B audience, personal values remain indicative of choices made about engagement. The stories shared will need to be different to create the progressive engagement that leads to consensus on purchase decisions.

Customer Experience Complexity

The complexity of digital strategies needed to create customer experiences should not be overlooked. Below is a sample list of the different components involved in crafting digital experiences. The various combinations are many. But what matters is creating the combinations that will deliver experiences that prospects and customers care about. While this is arguably based on the meaning the content establishes, the elements of personas, channels, content formats, and programs are what challenge marketers in the fluidity of overall experience.

One of the reasons why campaigns are so hard to give up is because their very structure creates a box that makes these components manageable for marketers. However, the resulting fragmentation does not bode well for a truly connected and contextual experience across the channels in which prospects and customers may choose to interact with your company. This is why a documented strategy is so important. Some of the research suggests that marketers with a documented strategy remain below the majority level. But those with a documented strategy outperform those without one. Execution without strategy is chaos. However, this does explain why companies are having such a difficult time endearing themselves to their customers.

Removing the silos that create fragmented digital customer experiences requires educating all roles on the customer lifecycle. For example, marketers

Personas	Channels	Content Formats	Programs
Decision Maker	Email	Email Copy	Lead Generation
Influencer(s)	Website	Articles	Demand Generation
Champion(s)	Blog	Blog Posts	Lead Nurturing
Gatekeeper	Social Media	Micro-Content	Public Relations
End User	Webinar	Video	Account Expansion
Customer(s)	Virtual Event	Infographic	Customer Retention
External Influencer(s)	Physical Event	White Paper	Customer Loyalty
Account(s)	Advertising	eBook	Vertical Specific
	SEO	Solution Brief	Newsletters
	Syndication	Datasheet	
	Sponsorships	Graphics	
	Partners/Resellers	Comparisons	
	Mobile	Native Advertising	

Figure 8.1 Components for Crafting Digital Experiences.

who are focused on demand generation only see one small piece of the customer journey. Without the ability to relate to the overall customer journey, the experiences they create for the sake of lead generation may set the wrong expectations or make less engaging promises to the types of people with the highest potential to become your customers. The same is true for social media functions that are solely focused on what's being said externally in relation to the brand. This lack of comprehensive customer understanding creates less than optimal experiences that do not promote consistency across channels.

What digital marketing teams need is the capability to think strategically across the end-to-end customer experience. But they also need the technology and budget to address the creating of better customer experiences given the complexity involved. And it's coming. According to Gartner, 22 percent of respondents in a recent study said that budget has been reallocated from sales to digital marketing because the buyers' path has changed. Thirty-one percent indicated that incremental funding is being obtained by other areas or business units, and 32 percent were able to gain net additional budget for digital marketing based on merit.[3]

Create Holistic Experiences for Customers

Digital strategies must reflect how the real world customers live in is evolving. Conversations, rather than a point in time, must be contiguous across the customer lifecycle. This requires a lot of coordination and a rethinking about go-to-market strategies. In the quest for relevance maturity, marketers must realize and embrace the fact that relevance can be learned, but to be effective, it must be earned.

Take a look at what the experience of a campaign might be like as a dialogue for your prospect:

Buyer: *I wonder what my peers are doing to address X?*

Marketer: *This email links to a blog post that shares six different ways people are dealing with X.*

Buyer: *That was great information. Oh look, they're having a webinar with more examples. I think I'll sign up.*

Marketer: *Thanks for attending our webinar. Here's a link to the replay.*

Buyer: *I was there. I don't need to see it again. What else have you got?*

Marketer: (Silence)

Buyer: *Hmm. Those examples in the webinar got me thinking, but I wonder if there are any industry best practices emerging about X?*

Marketer: (No response as the campaign is over for the marketer)

Buyer: *Where'd they go?*

Salesperson: *Since you attended our webinar, Marketer thought you might want a demo of our solution. Got 30 minutes? How about next Tuesday at 3 p.m.?*

Buyer: *What? I'm not even sure this will work for our situation. I need to talk to Kathy and David and Harvey and Sam...*

Salesperson: *I just sent you an email about a demo, thought I'd leave you a voicemail, too. Once you see our solution in action, you'll know we're the best choice.*

Buyer: *I wonder who the experts are who can help me learn more about dealing with X? Maybe I'll try asking my peers in a LinkedIn group discussion...*

Marketer: (Still no response as the campaign is over)

If you were in the buyer's shoes, would you feel left in the lurch about this topic that is of high interest to you? Would you be irritated at the salesperson's assumption? Would you do as the buyer in this scenario did and start looking for a more credible resource? I bet you would.

One of the reasons this happens is because most marketers don't see their program execution from the outside-in. When I speak at conferences and ask whether marketers go through their programs as their prospects or customers would, very few hands go up. But even if they do go through the motions, they think in terms of the campaign components, not the overall experience from their buyer's perspective. As long as the components are there, the campaign looks like the plan and it seems fine.

This is a big missed opportunity for gaining clarity about why the digital experiences you're creating are not delivering the levels of engagement and performance needed to move the needle. Or, if you're producing great experiences, going through the process as if you are the persona the campaign was designed to engage will help you learn how to replicate them. It's important to remember that what a campaign or execution plan or strategy looks like on paper can be much different in execution.

To create a holistic experience for customers, consider how this scenario differs from the one above:

Buyer: I wonder what my peers are doing to address X?

Marketer: This email links to a blog post that shares six different ways people are dealing with X.

Buyer: That was great information. Oh look, they're having a webinar with more

examples. I think I'll sign up.

Marketer: Thanks so much for attending our webinar. We've created a resource center with more information about best practices and insights to how industry trends are affecting X.

Buyer: Just what I need. This white paper is really helpful. Oh, it has a link to a thought leadership piece by one of their executives. This information will be great for my boss. Great, they've got a button to forward it.

Marketer: Since you downloaded our white paper, you might also be interested in this video where Sam, who has the same role as you, is talking about what they encountered during the implementation and how they overcame a few challenges to get the solution into production. Take a look.

Buyer: I was wondering about that. This is really helpful. I wonder if I can talk to this guy? I have a couple of questions.

Marketer: We're having a lunch and learn with Sam from the video you viewed. He'll be sharing more insights about how he got his team onboard and will be available for questions. And, we're serving a gourmet lunch. Let me know if you'd like to attend.

Buyer: I'll be there.

It's important to realize that this scenario would continue on for the buyer. Holistic experiences don't have an expiration date—they continue and renew based on the audience's place in the customer lifecycle. The components involved are complex, but putting the right foundation in place and monitoring continuously for responsiveness will help digital marketers to connect the dots for buyers and customers based on what they're interested in—not what their company wants to sell. Experiences that delight your audience must flow organically based on their behavior and digital expression. In the next chapter, you'll learn about this continuum approach and why it's the key to creating sustainable performance with digital strategies.

SECTION 3

The Need for a Continuum Approach

Marketing is no longer effective when it is comprised of one-off events, messages, or campaigns. The buying experience that leads to a complex purchase must be fluid, connected, and engaging across its entirety. Content marketing programs are the threads that weave together to create a fabric of engagement that accelerates pipeline velocity, putting salespeople in viable opportunity conversations sooner rather than later.

There are no stops and starts in a continuum. The flow is consistent, steady, and designed to build the problem-to-solution story with buyers by providing the education, expertise, and evidence they need to conclude that your company is the ultimate choice to help them achieve their business objectives. Taking a continuum approach will generate a transformation in marketing, from stand-alone efforts to integrated, continuous digital strategies that are proven to have a positive effect on revenue performance.

While many marketers have found it overwhelming to create the volume of relevant content they need to engage buyers, a continuum approach will help them learn to create efficiencies with content reinvention and expertise hubs that reduce the effort. Adapting to a continuum approach also takes a shift in mind-set and reinforcement to ensure it becomes a natural response to approaching marketing strategy.

Figure S3.1 The Digital Marketing Continuum.
Note: *Continuum – noun; A continuous extent, series or whole* - Dictionary.com

Removing the convenience of the boxed-in campaign approach opens up a lot of possibilities that can seem overwhelming at first. But once marketers adopt the conversational format, they 'll find that keeping the dialogue going is much easier to sustain than starting conversations from scratch with the launch of each new campaign.

CHAPTER 9

A Continuum Fuels Real-Time Relevance

The buyer has taken control of the purchasing process. This is a refrain heard often in marketing and sales channels. Information has become ubiquitous—as has access to it. No longer are companies and their salespeople the gatekeepers who must be sought out for help to assuage curiosity, reveal solutions to problems, build business cases, and select a short list of vendors to pursue. The informational gatekeepers are now represented by search engines, social networks, peers and colleagues, and perceptions of relevance.

Marketers and salespeople must be able to rely upon their ability to

- attract, keep, and develop the attention of buyers and influencers;
- engage with relevant and compelling information in the channels buyers prefer;
- create experiences based on context and what buyers and customers want and need;
- elevate the perceived value of every interaction—whether with marketing or sales.

A continuum must be sustained by stripping away the pretext, posturing, and limitations of traditional company and product-focused marketing. This approach is based on delivering value for buyers in every online interaction, at every stage, and with each touchpoint to create digital dialogues that drives sales momentum, continuing on across the entire customer lifecycle.

Where the continuum intersects with sales, the provision of value-added, fresh, and relevant ideas must seamlessly transition for prospects without interruption to momentum. Salespeople must be primed to provide unique expertise beyond what competitors can even imitate—should they try.

The ability to publish content online, interact with buyers, and engage in social conversations has become simple to execute. It's the planning, strategy, and context—along with a foundation for sustaining it consistently over time—that challenges marketers and salespeople. Shifting the dynamics of marketing requires new skills and ways of thinking. The following is a framework to help you prepare for sustainable marketing and sales efforts that put modern buyers and customers at the center of your strategy. Change is never easy, but it can certainly be transformative. Ready?

Get a Grip on the Publishing Imperative

Speed is one of the dynamics of digital marketing. The concept of real-time is pushing marketers to move more quickly than they've ever moved before. Speed for marketing is a construct driven by the ease of publishing content and the rallying cries of social media enthusiasts and so-called marketing gurus. Unfortunately, speed is also causing marketers to make brash moves that fragment their efforts as shiny new channels and tools urge them to do more, faster. This is not to say that marketers shouldn't take advantage of these new channels and capabilities, but that they need to take a deep breath and consider the implications to strategic business objectives that come with them.

Online publishing is a construct that can quickly spiral out of control—especially when mixed with speed. It covers every format for distributing content online, including, but in no way limited to, website content, articles, blog posts, video, white papers, case studies, eBooks, social media profiles, company pages on Facebook, LinkedIn discussions, forum questions and answers, webinars and virtual events, Tweets, podcasts, images, slide decks, and infographics. Let us not forget that online publishing also includes processes such as curating content and publishing press releases.

However, just because you can publish all of this stuff, doing so as random acts of marketing is not working. People share content they haven't read in social channels. The average duration on a web page is less than 15 seconds.[1] People read content and move on without developing any affinity for the brand that published it. Digital marketing cannot be approached with a *Field of Dreams* mind-set. It takes much more than publishing to entice people to become passionate about your ideas, embrace your company's expertise, or make the transition from viewing information to investing in your products to solve their problems.

One of the misconceptions that comes with speed is that it's an equal-opportunity dynamic. Just because marketers can publish content quickly doesn't mean that buyers will keep stride with this breakneck pace. The rise in content publishing assumes that there's a corresponding rise in the availability of time and attention needed to consume that volume of content. For buyers, often the opposite is true. Marketers may be producing more content, but buyers often have less time to consume it. Given this constraint, they definitely have less patience for irrelevance.

Three Factors That Impact the Buying Experience

- **Finding the right information:** The overwhelming amount of information available on every topic imaginable makes it more difficult for buyers to filter it to determine which is credible, or even useful. The time this takes is also limited, slowing the buying process, regardless of how fast marketers think they're addressing buyers' needs by publishing more information at a rapid pace—even if it's information that buyers know they need. Rather than publishing more, we need to work on how to make sure that the content we're developing gets found.
- **Convincing the right people:** In a complex buying process, more people must reach consensus—each of them with differing priorities and motivations. The content that works to convince one stakeholder to embrace the proposed change may not work to persuade the others.
- **Building the best business case:** Today's economic climate has changed the usual budgetary structure, requiring buyers to identify problems, the reasons for solving them and—only once that foundation has been established—to build a business case to secure the budget to proceed. Research by DemandGen Report found that 34 percent of B2B purchases were made in this fashion by the buyers surveyed.[2]

All three of these factors can be answered with digital marketing, but to do so, marketers must first plan for and address the challenge of being found in the channels your prospects prefer. Most importantly, the content published must be relevant enough to sustain attention over the entirety of the buying process. It is through the ability to create ongoing engagement with information that is crucial to each stakeholder on the buying committee that will reveal the value of the continuum approach to produce proactive buyers in shorter time frames.

CHAPTER 10

Creating a Continuum Approach

Engaging prospects across the entirety of the purchasing process and customer lifecycle must become the goal of marketers. In today's online business environment, this means not only the ability to create relevant, two-way, digital dialogues but to sustain them over the long term. By flipping your focus from the way your company defines the sales process to how buyers engage in the buying experience, you'll gain a better understanding of how to make this happen.

Instead of sticking with a traditional funnel constructed with an inside-out sales perspective and based on some kind dwindling percentage formula that narrows the field, focus the stages of the process on the continuum experience with an outside-in perspective. When this experience is created based on meeting the needs of all the stakeholders involved in the decision, you'll see a swelling in the middle, instead of the constriction that indicates fallout, or leakage, in a traditional funnel.

In Figure 10.1, notice the buyer/customer and marketing are interwoven throughout the entire buying experience—and beyond. Salespeople enter the process around the fifth stage, Buying Committee Involvement, and are usually out of the equation after the buyer purchase.

Most importantly, recognize the expansion that happens in the middle of the continuum experience during buying committee involvement. This is where knowing who else is involved in the process—and addressing their interests—is critical to continuing the flow of buying momentum. The modern buying experience is quite different from the process most marketers have enabled and supported in the past.

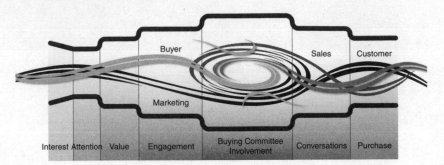

Figure 10.1 The Continuum Experience.

A disconnected experience may occur because marketers haven't changed in response to how their buyers have shifted. This failure to shift is also reflected in lower relevance. Research conducted by IDG Connect finds that up to 30 percent of digital assets either misalign with what buyers value, misstate the value, or miss actually stating the value at all.[1] Research by the CMO Council into what buyers' value in terms of content includes breadth and depth of information, ease of access, and originality of thinking.[2] This is not the type of content conducive to a speed-first approach.

It's also prudent to note that marketers don't rate their effectiveness with digital marketing as very effective—only 40 percent of marketers asked think their company's marketing is effective. Although 66 percent of the same marketers think companies won't succeed unless they have a digital marketing approach.[3] But marketers do realize that improving the experiences they deliver is imperative. Personalization ranked the highest when marketers were asked to prioritize one capability that will be most important in moving their company's marketing forward.[4] Addressing the entire experience in a continuous, consistent, and increasingly relevant manner presents a huge opportunity for digital marketers.

The continuum approach has a direct overlay to the stages of the buying process and the questions your prospects will need to have answered as they move from stage to stage.

Note the parallels between the buyer experience, the buying stages, and the corresponding buyer questions in Figure 10.2. There is a fluency of progression from the top to the bottom in each column. Each row relates the mind-set for the overlay of the experience with the buying stage and the type of questions to be answered. Addressing this combination when designing

Buyer Experience	Buying Stages	Buyer Questions
Interest: I'm curious enough to take a look.	**Status Quo:** Problem not yet recognized as painful enough to fix.	Why should I care?
Attention: I like what I see so far.	**Priority:** Problem recognized but unsure how to proceed.	What should I know?
Value: This can really help me achieve goals.	**Research:** Actively engaged in learning what they need to know to take action.	What are best practices?
Engagement: I need to find out more about how they deliver what they promise.	**Options:** Identifying solution sets that can provide the most value for now and future.	Who has the expertise?
Buying Committee Involvement: Everyone needs to get on board.	**Step backs:** Stops to verify beliefs or find answers to new questions	What if...?
Conversations: I want to make sure I can work with you – trust you.	**Validation:** Exploring evidence that supports vendor promises.	Why should I believe you?
Purchase	**Choice:** Deciding to buy.	You'll bring the most value

Figure 10.2 The Overlays in the Buyer's Journey.

your continuum approach will result in increased relevance when matched to the specifics of your company's personas.

Prospect Attention Is Earned in Stages

Attention is the capacity to maintain selective or sustained concentration. The amount of attention your prospects attribute to your digital dialogue will be indicative of their propensity to buy from your company. A digital continuum helps marketers develop the best buyer experience, with the goal of owning as much attention from your target markets as possible. But it's important to consider that earning and sustaining attention must establish progression across all stages of the buying process. The level of your relevance maturity will also influence how well you're able to convince prospects to pay the highest level of attention to you—the type of attention that is needed to convert prospects into customers.

As you create a digital continuum strategy to provide a compelling buying experience, determine which types of attention you could be attracting and how you'll be able to make advances in the stages of attention with the dialogue you're developing.

Cursory attention—This type of attention is the equivalent of curiosity in the Interest stage of the continuum experience. This is your buyer telling you that he may be interested in what you have to say, but is thus far unconvinced of how much of his time your content and dialogue warrant.

This is status quo and is where you start as your prospects find your company and content. If you do not capitalize on this opportunity, the bar is raised exponentially to create the level of engagement necessary to sustain attention and develop it across the continuum of the buying experience.

Misleading attention—The buyer thought she was interested, but her attention wandered. She may possibly still be staring at your content, but thinking that she needs to pick up her dry cleaning on the way home from work or wondering what her husband wants for dinner.

Misleading attention can also be gained from people who want a content offer for the information it promises, but not because they're interested in buying from you. Unfortunately, it is at this stage of attention that many prospects are considered leads and handed over to the sales team. This is a premature action that can cost you the attention progress you've made if the salesperson makes the assumption that the prospect is an opportunity and chooses to proceed with a pitch.

Voluntary attention—At this stage of attention are the people who subscribe to everything you publish. They read your blog, sign up to attend webinars, but always stop short of taking the next step that would indicate momentum in the buying process. This said, this is the type of attention that results in earned media, referrals, and advocates, so it's wise to cultivate it.

This level of attention can also indicate bottlenecks in the middle of the buying process between engagement and buying committee involvement. If you see stalling in the buying process, it could well indicate that action should be taken to prompt a move to the next stage. It may also indicate where a gap in your story line exists, with the next step asking for too much of a leap of faith the prospect isn't yet confident enough to take. Closing that gap can help prospects reach the next level of attention.

Intentional attention—BINGO! This is the type of attention you want to achieve. These are the buyers who are intent on learning what they need to know to make a purchase decision. They interact purposefully with your content and proactively access it, even without prompting from nurturing emails or social posts. You can see a pattern in the content they're accessing and the dialogue in which they participate or follow.

These are the buyers who will invite sales into conversations when they reach the options stage in their buying process. However, by arming salespeople with highly relevant content related to the issues buyers have expressed an interest in resolving—based on their pattern of content engagement—marketers can help salespeople step into the conversation fully prepared to add the value that buyers crave.

Owning attention requires patience and perseverance. It is related to trust and credibility, both of which are reliant upon relevance maturity. Attention is critical to the buying experience. Without it, buying from your company won't happen. By understanding that attention develops in stages, it becomes easier to build this escalation into the continuum from the beginning.

The Importance of Integrating Distribution Channels

With the increasing comfort buyers have for sourcing information online and participating in social media—not to mention using search engines and personalized filters, such as Flipboard, Zite, and LinkedIn Pulse—the quality of your digital dialogue must be impeccable. It's imperative that your digital marketing programs show buyers the consistency and expertise that demonstrate the traits of a partner they'd choose to help them solve their highest-priority problems, as well as to protect their careers from unnecessary risk.

Online publishing has enabled marketers to expand the distribution channels they use to share content and reach buyers. Unfortunately, the norm is that these channels are executed as silos, rather than as one comprehensive program. Sometimes this is due to how marketing tasks are distributed across the company. Sometimes it's simply that no strategy exists to execute channels in sync with overall objectives and goals. And sometimes, there's just not enough insight or attention paid to how a prospect's experience will change from channel to channel.

This needs to change for the sake of relevance. And change quickly. Ask yourself the following questions:

- When's the last time I typed my company's name into a search engine?
- What are the keywords and phrases my buyers use?
- Have I experienced my marketing programs as my buyers do?

Let's say that your company has a website, an expertise micro-site, a company blog, several employees who both Tweet and blog personally, a group on LinkedIn, a YouTube channel, and nurturing programs designed to engage three personas. These channels are executed by three different marketing groups: demand generation, web marketing, and social media.

How likely is it that each of these three marketing groups knows what the others are doing? The reality is that prospects will traverse a variety of channels during their research for problem solving and searching for the expertise they need to achieve objectives. In the scenario above, prospects are likely to encounter content and dialogue placed online by each of the three groups. Will their experience be consistent? Or will the contrast be so fragmented that attention wanes, resulting in a diminishing level of interest in doing business with your company?

Each channel requires a unique format, tone, and style of content. The key is to make sure that the message experience is consistent, connected, and relevant, encouraging a higher level of engagement and intent with every interaction.

Capitalize on the Digital Continuum

As digital channels and social platforms become more embedded in business, marketers and salespeople alike must become proficient with the skills necessary to address their company's strategic objectives. The ability for buyers and customers to exchange information interactively with their peers, colleagues, and partners will only increase. This reality can be extremely liberating for buyers, but it also serves to introduce confusion by stretching their ability to filter information to determine what is credible and what— and whom—they should ignore.

This informational flow never stops. Therefore, marketing and sales must be diligent, consistent, and continuous in their efforts to interact with the people who can benefit the most from the products and solutions their companies provide. Sustainable marketing and sales programs that deliver on objectives must put buyers at the center of strategy.

With a continuum approach, marketers and salespeople can collaboratively build the foundation needed to successfully

- be found with the right information in the channels buyers prefer;
- attract, sustain, and escalate the attention of buyers and influencers;
- respond appropriately with digital relevance that motivates buyer intent;
- elevate the perceived value of every interaction—whether with marketing or sales.

By knowing your buyers and understanding their needs, preferences, priorities, and aversions, marketers and salespeople can provide the education, expertise, and evidence needed to become strategic resources and the partners that buyers choose to engage with and buy from.

It's time to make the move from static to dynamic. There's no going back.

CHAPTER 11

Moving from Campaign to Continuum

I nvestopedia defines a marketing campaign as "specific activities designed to promote a product, service or business."[1] Campaigns are an inside-out construct based on what the company wants to achieve—namely, sales. That the action of a campaign is to "promote" is indicative of a traditional marketing mindset that doesn't translate well to a customer-driven digital environment. Campaigns are indicative of irrelevance or shifting relevance on the RMM.

Campaigns have a number of limitations, some of which are

- start and end dates,
- attempts to compress the buying experience based on the company's agenda,
- a lack of alignment with prospects,
- reliance on content that includes obvious vendor bias,
- a lack of contextual personalization.

Back when distributing content was based mostly on media buys and paid channel placement or syndication, marketers were in control of the information flow. This allowed a certain amount of freedom to decide what to promote to whom and when and how to do so. Marketers called the shots on timing, and there was little competitive pressure for producing a volume of content. A little content could go a long way because there wasn't much competing with it.

The rise of the digital environment has made those traditional marketing assertions irrelevant. Once content became freely available and anyone (buyer or seller) could create and post their own content, the floodgates opened. As publishing became easy, marketers took up the challenge. Some of them did so successfully, and some not so much.

Marketing Is about Much More Than Publishing

Think like a publisher! That's been the rallying cry for content marketing for the last few years. But digital marketing requires a whole lot more than publishing—especially for companies with complex sales.

Many companies that have taken up the rallying cry have produced some pretty good content, but it's still often based on random acts of publishing. This means, there's no apparent strategy behind it. Most of the content I see does nothing to orchestrate buyer progression and next steps. The repetitive, shallow nature of much of the content published lacks the relevance of specificity for target audience needs and priorities.

Only 42 percent of B2B marketers saying they're effective at content marketing, and the focus on publishing over substance and strategy has a lot to do with this. Only 44 percent of marketers say they have a documented strategy, even though 73 percent say their companies do have someone who oversees content marketing strategy.[2] Yes, this confused me, too.

But looking beyond this, the same research finds that 68 percent of marketers are focused on thought leadership as an organizational goal. This is another conundrum as the meaning of the concept has become shallow with misplaced use. As evidence of this, people may be reading or viewing the content that digital marketers produce, but then they just move on. The quality and relevance of the content isn't high enough to motivate action or sway opinion. In essence, marketers' focus on publishing has been focused on the act, rather than the meaning.

The common issues with random acts of content include the following:

- **There is too much focus on the company's perspective rather than the buyer's.**
  Does your content show that you really understand what your buyers care about? Or have you made assumptions that leave your content short on quality and perceived relevance? Do your products sneak into your content? How about feeds and speeds? Do you use "we" and "our" more than "you" and "your"?

- **There is no call to action.**

  What comes next after the content the buyer has just viewed? Do you show them? Your audience is not going to go looking for what's next. They'll just move on once they're finished reading what's in front of them. People are often multitasking when viewing content. You have to give them a reason to spend more than cursory attention on your content. And it should be so obvious that they can't miss it.

- **It is perceived that too much effort is required to take the suggested action.**

  Does the form you present for downloading a content offer ask for the kitchen sink? Do you only offer a video link without a transcript for those who prefer to read? Are you trying to send your audience to a different channel that they don't use or a place where they have to set up an account to gain access? The need for too much effort can manifest in many different ways, but it usually results in the audience moving on to something that is perceived as easier.

- **There are gaps in the story—also known as leaps of faith.**

  When I ask marketers the last time they experienced their content as if they were their buyers, most of them can't say they have done so. They often think they've covered all the bases, but they are stuck with the curse of knowledge. Marketers know the whole story and think it's reflected in their content. But often, it is not. Because they don't have a strategy, they haven't orchestrated the story. The outcome is that they may be asking their buyers to leap from one concept to the next without any foundation. This is a problem that costs the company in credibility and in progressive engagement with buyers. This type of experience is also high-effort.

- **No one takes ownership of expertise.**

  A lot of content doesn't take a stand because it's trying to make everyone happy. But that's not the point of effective content. The sharing of expertise must be done with authority and through confident ideas that help people with specific roles, responsibilities, and problems visualize what your expertise will bring to the table that they can't get elsewhere. Show them you mean what you say and feel strongly about it. Tell them why. Make your case.

- **Content stays at too high a level.**

  Phrases like "grow revenues" or "cut costs" can mean anything. Content that motivates action must take a deep dive into the specifics applicable to the audience it's intended to sway. Quite often it just does a white-wash across the benefits. This approach does nothing to differentiate your company or your expertise.

- **Content is not targeted to a specific audience.**

  This is why a lot of content stays at a high level. Marketers don't know their audiences well enough to get into the nitty-gritty. But, if you don't get to know them, they won't go on their buying journey with you. They'll go find a competitor who delivers more value and helps them visualize their problem being solved.

Publishing content is necessary. Marketers need to do this to attract and engage buyers. But an editorial calendar with a list of random topics you think are interesting won't cut the mustard. Quarterly themes won't do it either. All the switching around will just alienate people who were finally getting invested in the story you were telling last quarter.

Random acts of publishing won't get the level of engagement and intention needed to move the needle because you won't be able to sustain it long enough to help buyers learn what they need to know to choose to have a one-to-one conversation.

What you need is a digital strategy. A strategy produces a method for the madness that is solving complex problems. With a continuum approach it is a plan for strategic storytelling across channels orchestrated to create momentum in the buying process. There's much more to content marketing than publishing.

Why Campaigns Don't Work

Campaigns are the equivalent of ADD for marketing. Marketers are so familiar with their content that they get bored. But they fail to realize that their buyers may not be bored; or that they haven't seen the content or become convinced to buy. Campaigns lack commitment so it's easy to flip your focus to some other trendy topic and head off down another path with each new campaign created. Take a look at the average length of time it takes to move a prospect from lead to customer. Companies with complex sales usually have longer cycles that can range from nine months to several years. With this in mind, just how effective do you think a 3-month campaign executed over a calendar quarter will be? Do you see the disconnect?

Consider the impressions that campaigns can leave with your buyers:

- Disappointment that content they were interested in has reached a conclusion without providing them all the insight they needed to make an informed decision
- Confusion about the actual value your company provides
- Diminishing relevance that results in their attention moving elsewhere to get what they need

Put yourself in your buyers' shoes and imagine you're trying to solve a specific problem.

- You find an article that speaks to that problem and follow the link to the website
- You register for and download a related white paper while you're there
- Over the course of several months you receive related information from the company that helps you learn more about what you need to know. But you still have questions and need to convince the other members of the buying committee that this company can help.
- Next month you get an email promoting the value of a different product. This is a sure sign that one campaign ended and another one began. But you're not done with your research and evaluation yet. The business case isn't built and you haven't been able to convince all the stakeholders to reach consensus. In fact, you're nowhere near ready to do this.

From the buyers' perspective, how interested are you now?

The Difference with a Continuum Approach

Creating a continuum starts with personas that help marketers take what they know about target markets to an extreme. The reason this is important is that a continuum approach doesn't end. It continues across the entire customer lifecycle, focused on achieving goals at each stage. Think of it this way; with a campaign you have a fixed goal to achieve in a set period of time. With a continuum you have many goals to achieve over the customer lifecycle and the latitude to tweak and refine them as new knowledge and buyer insights become available. Instead of once and done, you're in a state of continuous improvement of the "wheel," rather than reinventing it with each campaign launch.

Giving up campaigns is difficult. Some of this has to do with accountability. Since campaigns are apples and oranges, marketers are only accountable for the campaigns in play at the time of the report or performance evaluation. Campaigns have different components and different agendas. One may be to generate leads, one to build awareness and another to drive web traffic. The success of one may not be tied to the others. A campaign is its own little box, often without attention paid to any others in the market at the same time.

With a continuum, marketers are accountable for demonstrating improvement in performance since their last report. A continuum helps to establish consistent key performance indicators (KPIs) that you report against each period—apples to apples. It is also a construct that encompasses all of your efforts across channels. It leads to integrated thinking and consistency that prospects and customers will both appreciate.

A continuum is also about orchestration over the long-term. Because everything is connected to what's next and what's come before, it leads prospects to more relevant information once they've selected something they're interested in. With analytics in place, marketers can now begin to identify patterns of content consumption and digital activity that are indicative of intentional attention and propensity to buy.

The result? More highly qualified buyers that salespeople will clamor to pursue. Longer and more profitable customer relationships that help create sustainable growth for your company.

CHAPTER 12

Get More Value from Investments in Content

Great content is an investment and should be considered an asset, rather than an expense. With a continuum approach, content becomes integral to the story that's being shared with each target audience. Because the story is targeted and told continuously, your content should evolve over time, not used once and tossed aside for the next new piece. Marketers are involved with all the content they create for digital continuum strategies. They've seen it all, so it's easy to believe that everyone else has seen it, too. But they haven't. Not even close. Even with hundreds or thousands of views, it's likely that you're only scratching the surface of the content's lifetime value.

With a continuum approach, content can be thought of as building blocks rather than campaign-specific pieces to be used once and archived. Given the difficulties that marketers have with finding enough time to produce content, as well as the effort required to produce relevant content, reinvention, repurposing, and repetition can become your ace in the hole for providing consistent support for the execution of your continuum strategy.

Here are three ways to get more from your investment in content:

Reinvention: Content that currently exists must be audited and reimagined to provide coverage in more than one channel. Often, marketers will create a big asset, such as a white paper, use it once in a lead generation campaign, and then relegate it to the resources section of the corporate website. With all the new channels in the marketing mix, marketers can use that white paper for much more.

For example:

- Pull a chart used in a white paper and write a bit of commentary addressing the findings and post it to the corporate blog. Link back to the white paper to encourage more downloads.
- White papers are usually written in sections. Pull each section and turn it into a stand-alone article. Use the articles as a series for a nurturing program or in your monthly newsletter. Hyperlink to them from related areas on your website to create a connected chapter of the story.
- Tweet with a related #hashtag to expand the reach of the white paper, blog post, and articles.
- Use the white paper as the basis for a slide deck you can share on Slideshare as well as embed in a blog post or a related section on the corporate website.
- Create another version of the slide deck to host a webinar on the topic. Transform sections of the webinar that cover a point or topic into a podcast.
- If the white paper includes research, create an infographic that you can post on your blog and share via social channels. Including an embed code can encourage others with similar audiences to share it via their blogs. Make sure to include sources for the research to increase your company's credibility and potentially expand exposure if your infographic is linked to as the source when someone else references one of the statistics in their content.

Repurposing: As has been discussed previously, content is more effective when its focus is narrowed to address the needs of one target segment. What may not be readily apparent is that there may be overlays across industries, or segments.

- Take a look at your persona—or target segment—questions to see if versions of the same question are asked by different personas. It may be that a content asset designed for one persona can be quickly revised to answer the version of the question asked by another.
- Many companies address the same target audience in a variety of vertical industries. Make the appropriate changes to the content to position it for each industry where it applies. I will caution you that just changing

the references to the industry is not enough. Make sure to address the subtle differences and phrasing to express your understanding of each industry and audience.

Repetition: Marketers should frame the context for repetition by using the ideas shared in their content more than once. New ideas require time to take hold. Ideas may need to be presented in a variety of ways to create "light bulb" moments for the various perspectives of the intended audience.

Here's a basic example. Let's say the main idea is "The expectations of the new buyer." The original idea is to write an article about how the buyer has changed, backed up with industry statistics and examples that are relevant for the target market you've selected.

To put repetition into play, determine other ways to spin this main idea. Examples might include

- ten reasons you need to change what you're telling buyers;
- why your customer's trust level has declined—and how to reverse the trend;
- how to have an online conversation with today's digitally empowered buyer;
- what salespeople need in order to provide value that persuades the new buyer.

Now you have five topics based on one main idea that you can develop into marketing content using the same research you'll do to develop the content asset around the main idea, all with a different take or spin, each one reinforcing your expertise on the topic.

It's important to take note that repetition can go horribly wrong if not used properly.

Repetition is not

- **using the same piece of content over and over with the same messaging.** Blasting the same email copy multiple times to your database is redundant and irritating. Marketers may think that if an "open" isn't indicated, then their prospects haven't seen it. But many no longer automatically download pictures when previewing email, so it's more likely that it's been seen and discarded than that it has just slipped by them unnoticed. Switch it up and write the email copy from a different angle, and use a new subject line to find out if a new approach will produce greater results from those who have not clicked the link.

- **saying the same things everyone else in your market is saying.** When attention intensifies, concepts become buzzwords and topics du jour, such as Cloud, Big Data, and Content Marketing. Everyone jumps on the bandwagon and wants to present their take to gain attention. Entering the search term "big data" into Google, for example, will return versions of "What Is Big Data?" articles from SAS, Oracle, IBM, and a slew of others. They're all really saying the same thing. Who of us hasn't seen a multitude of articles about why you need content marketing? Or, the many list posts for the elements needed for the perfect blog post. They're practically interchangeable. Content that's interchangeable does not differentiate your brand.

- **using the same self-serving calls to action.** While contact information that's easily accessible to prospects and customers is important, continuously pushing them to "Schedule a Demo Today!" or "Have a Salesperson Contact Me" come across as pushy when prominently displayed on all content, regardless of the prospect's stage in the buying process. Repetition of self-serving calls to action will eventually convince prospects that selling to them is all you care about. Instead, become more innovative and suggest topics for discussion for conversations based on problem solving and sharing new ideas, rather than sales.

- **repeated posts to social media using the title and link.** Many people have espoused the idea that the balance for social media posts should be 4–1–1. This guidance suggests a ratio of four posts of other people's content to one promotional post and one post linking to company-produced content. Following some ratio like this will keep marketers from appearing too self-focused, but if the company-focused posts repeat the same title + link to content format again and again, it can look as if your company has nothing else to say. One way to mix it up is to develop a slate of social media posts when you create the content, each one different. This will keep your profiles on social media from appearing boring and repetitive.

Address Your Buyers' Learning Styles

Your buyers will find some content more compelling, depending on their preferences for learning information. Some people are visual and need to "see" or be able to visualize the meaning of your content. Others are auditory learners who understand by "hearing" the information, and a third group is predisposed toward kinesthetic learning or "feeling" the story you're sharing.

Obviously, formats such as videos, infographics, and webinars can work for both audio and visual learners. But so can text-based content. Word choice is important and offers yet another way to spin your story to appeal to different types of people who are your buyers.

Note the difference in these word choices:

- visual: see, look, view, visualize, imagine
- audio: hear, listen, tune-in, sound, resonate
- kinesthetic: feel, hard, soft, touch, hold

The words your buyers use can help you understand their preferred learning style. But so can the content with which they spend the most time engaging. By spinning versions of your content to employ a specific type—visual, audio, or kinesthetic—of words, you can attract the buyer most engaged by the words you use. Make sure to use them in the title and description as well, to allow your audience to quickly assess relevance on this level.

Creating content that speaks to learning styles will help prospects with different preferences assign a higher level of relevance to your content— whether by format or by textual style. Look for patterns in their behavior that will help you determine whether styles are similar for people assigned to specific persona tracks.

Connecting the Dots with Content

Getting more value from your content is also predicated by how strategic storytelling is used to connect the dots for your buyers. In this sense, it's not about getting more use out of your marketing content, but about using it better. While it would be much easier for us as marketers if buyers would enter their buying process with us by using our status quo content and then following along as we unfold the story in a linear fashion, that's no longer the reality of how buyers buy.

The ability to stay anonymous longer in the buying process makes it more difficult for marketers to determine just what stage the buyer is in once they identify themselves. For example, a prospect may have already determined by the time she finds your company and your content that her status quo situation needs to change. Whether or not your content plays a role in challenging her status quo, it's important to attract buyers during the early stages, before a competitor has become the "anchor" for their thinking about how to solve the problem they face.

Combining content in different ways can help you gain insight into the context of the buyer, as well as allow you alternative methods for building engagement. An example could be to offer both the piece of the story that precedes the content they're viewing, as well as the content that represents what follows. The path they choose can be indicative of what they need to learn, and hence where they are in their buying process.

One of the best ways to learn what your buyers are most interested in is to create expertise or topic hubs. The problem with most corporate websites is that information is most commonly presented in silos. A standard main navigation may include About Us, Solutions, Services, Industries, Customers, Resources, and Contact Us. Your buyer is required to hop around from one section to another to search for the information they're looking for in order to see each piece of the puzzle they are trying to solve.

This type of self-serve experience is difficult for marketers to make sense of in analytics or to draw insights from that help them improve the relevance and engagement of their content offers. But, if we create pages or hubs of topical information, we're serving up choices that make sense in relation to the topic.

As an example, Forrester does this well with its solutions pages. Figure 12.1 is a screenshot of this analyst firm's Empowered Customers page.[1]

This page offers content specific to marketers and to technology managers about why it's important to them to become customer obsessed to gain competitive advantage. It also provides choices of four market imperatives that Forrester wants to help companies learn more about. When a visitor to this page makes a content selection, Forrester can learn quite a bit, from the role the visitor selects as well as the imperative that he displays the most interest in.

The grouping of content is all related to the topic of the page. Forrester shares its expertise not only to engage website visitors in a topic of interest but

Figure 12.1 A Forrester Content Hub.

also to show the breadth of its expertise in this area. By presenting a variety of related content with this page serving as the umbrella over the four hubs they've developed for the imperatives, their relevance goes up and the website visitor's effort goes down. The page is clean and engaging, and allows for the visitor to orient themselves quickly and choose what to view with one click.

In a conversation I had with Jeff Ernst, VP of Marketing at Forrester, he confirmed that the web pages were created as hubs for marketing activities. The hubs are built, managed, and hosted on the Ion Interactive LiveBall platform that provides tools for A/B testing, short links, intermediate capture of contacts via forms, and also double posts to Eloqua for monitoring and connecting prospect activity.

The content in the hubs also serves as a resource for the company, and links to the pages are included by the analysts in blog posts they've written on similar subjects, as well as to share the content on social platforms. When asked about the performance of the hubs, Ernst shared with me that the hubs were rolled out beginning with Customer Experience in June 2013, then Digital Disruption, and Mobile later in the summer, and the Age of the Customer in December 2013. From June 2013 to April 2014—only nine months—the hubs pulled 133K unique visitors, nearly 9K of which completed a form for a content offer. After the company matched the contacts to its ideal customer profile, it found that nearly half are viable marketing leads.

Ernst says that Forrester has drastically reduced spending on purchased lists, paid media, and advertising. The cost of creating the hubs was minimal in comparison to the costs of either of those options. This is because content is not in short supply at Forrester. Intelligence presented in the form of content is the firm's product.

Ernst says they took a new approach when the book *The Mobile Mind Shift*, written by Forrester Analysts Ted Schadler, Josh Bernoff, and Julie Ask, was published in June 2014. They updated the Mobile imperative content hub web page to feature the book, additional content resources, and created interactive engagement on Twitter using the hashtag #MyMobileMoment. According to Ernst, nearly 1,000 people had shared mobile moments at the time of our conversation.

CoreMedia, a client that provides web content management solutions, chose to create a persona-driven consensus hub on its website for the launch of CoreMedia 7. The company created a series of videos based on the personas to which it sells. Five videos in which actors played the personas were created for a total cost of $35K. Each persona video plays on its own page with content designed around topics that resonate for that persona. The videos are designed to represent what the buying committee process might entail for each role that is involved. The final video is the consensus meeting. Figure 12.2 is a screenshot of the hub for Online Managers on the CoreMedia website.[2]

When I spoke with Glenn Conradt, Vice President of Global Marketing and North America for CoreMedia recently, he said that the response to the hub has been much greater than they'd expected and that by providing people with the option of choosing to whom they relate most, engagement has increased. They have been able to match website visitors and prospects more easily to personas for marketing efforts, which isn't always simple given the array of titles in use globally. Conradt said that it's been a challenge to pivot the organization to customer-first thinking, but that he's encouraged by the

Figure 12.2   CoreMedia Persona Content Hub.

progress. Recently he asked his web team to audit older content against the company's personas, and said they were "blown away" by the differences they identified.

One of the things Conradt found most interesting during the hub project is that the German side of the company insisted that the persona videos wouldn't work in Germany. In reality, however, the videos have performed very well there. The intelligence gathered from a more personalized approach to content and communications is helping the organization to continue to iterate its way of thinking. CoreMedia is intent on continuing to shift the focus of its content to what its prospects and customers care about most. Conradt said that due to the success to date, the way the organization enables its partners is being reevaluated, based on the same persona methodology.

His team is finding ways to apply the outside-in approach beyond just content creation to experiences and empowerment they can enable for different constituencies.

There are many different ways to connect the dots for buyers through content presentation. Part of the strategic effort of designing a continuum approach for digital marketing is in determining the best options for engagement scenarios. While marketers need to present highly relevant content to attract buyers, they also must present it in ways that enable analytics to depict patterns of interest that can be used to increase and sustain engagement. Once you know how a buyer is engaging in the story, it becomes simpler to predict more accurately what should be presented to them next to continue their momentum toward a profitable customer relationship.

SECTION 4

Storytelling—Make Your Customer the Hero

S torytelling is part art, part science. Using personas as characters and solving the business problem as the structure for a plot, marketers can learn how to develop a business story structure that fuels the continuum approach to digital marketing. By becoming adept at weaving stories together across channels, marketers can also increase their capability to connect with buyers wherever an opportunity arises.

It's become clear that buyers are in the power position during the buying process. Yet, I still hear marketers who refer to their companies or products as the hero of the story. There's no dancing around this. Those marketers have missed the point.

The hero of the story is the protagonist or main character. The protagonist has a goal, is impeded by the antagonist/villain in achieving the goal, seeks knowledge along the way from a mentor to vanquish the villain, and achieves victory to accomplish his goal successfully at the end. Do you see anywhere in this overview of a story where your product fits? No, I thought not.

To transform a fictional story into a business story structure, try this:

The buyer (hero) has a business objective (goal), is impeded by problems or issues (villain) that get in the way of achieving it. The buyer seeks knowledge along the way aided by vendor expertise (mentor) and achieves his objective with the help of your product to solve the problems and issues in order to find success (victory).

Now, let's apply this approach to a potential real-world business buyer. We'll start with the backstory to illustrate the type of insights into buyers that's needed to develop a story where they play the role of the hero. Your personas should include this type of information.

A chief technology officer (CTO) and founder of a start-up software-as-a-service (SaaS) company that's the subsidiary of a global enterprise is building a new application with a business model that depends upon low price, high volume sales. He knows that, at launch, the delivery and support of his application must be rock solid, the site streamlined and responsive—regardless of how much traffic hits it. This is a key product launch for the parent company, with a lot riding on it, including the CTO's career.

He's formed a great core team focused on the development of this innovative application. He is trying to decide how to support taking the application to market.

The options he's identified include

- *building the infrastructure in-house, which includes hiring the team, buying the hardware, developing the network, colocating the servers, and so forth;*
- *building it in-house and spinning up the servers from Google or AWS to host it in the cloud, which also means hiring the team to build and support it;*
- *outsourcing the infrastructure to a managed services provider and keeping his team's focus solely on core product development, delivery, and service.*
- *employing the services of his parent company's IT division to support roll out, which is the option his parent company would prefer and which his board is pushing for;*
- *using the vendors his parent company uses to try and find economies of scale, which may be easier for his parent company to swallow than choosing to use new, unproven vendors.*

Some of his concerns include

- *having an accelerated launch date, which means he has to get the infrastructure up faster than he'd planned;*
- *addressing concern about security and compliance in the cloud, as his research shows that his customers will have a certain level of discomfort with a cloud-based deployment;*

- *feeling a reluctance to split his or his team's time between innovations for the new product and managing the infrastructure;*
- *scaling the infrastructure if volume grows faster than forecast;*
- *having a lack of confidence that the managed services vendors will do more than "dial it in" after the contract is signed (based on past experience);*
- *controlling costs to keep slim margins in the acceptable range for the board;*
- *minimizing any perceptions that will get in the way of his potential customers embracing this new application.*

If you are a cloud managed services provider, how will you build the story for this buyer?

Will you tell him that the cloud is the hero that will save the day because you're the leading provider of cloud services?

Or will you

- share deep insights about the challenges of taking a new SaaS product to market and how cloud compares to an on-premise deployment for scale, uptime, responsiveness, and rolling out product updates;
- produce content that talks about the role a managed services team plays in collaborating with the core team to make sure the infrastructure supports new product developments and customer demands;
- help him understand how the security and compliance measures you can provide will be a selling point for his customers—and his executive board;
- show him how a "pay for what you use" model will help him keep margins where they need to be;
- share your insights about how the future trends you see for the industry will be easier to address with a cloud infrastructure and why this is important for his app and his customers when it comes time to scale.

There are many angles your story can take and a number of chapters to unfold that will be integral to helping the buyer build the trust and credibility he needs to take the risk of choosing to use an outside vendor, let alone the cloud. The CTO will need a lot of information to build the business case and drive consensus with his board and parent company. But the story must first focus on convincing the CTO that choosing your company is his best option given the choices he could make for deploying this new application.

None of the stories this buyer needs revolve around your product or solution as the hero. Your solution is simply one component of the business the buyer is building. The story you need to share is one that increases the buyer's confidence that he's making the best, lowest risk choice that will lead to his SaaS application succeeding in the marketplace, as well as to elevating his career.

This is the nature of business storytelling. Because a business story is focused on the entire buying experience, it is perfectly suited as the strategic baseline for a highly relevant digital marketing continuum approach.

CHAPTER 13

Our Brains on Stories—Why Stories Work

S tories have been around forever. Stories are the way we interpret and make sense of our world, the way we communicate with others, and the way we justify the decisions we make. Storytelling is the most powerful method we have for attracting and keeping the attention of others and of connecting with them emotionally—whether personally or professionally. It is also the most compelling way to transfer knowledge. Facts are important, but unless they are woven into a compelling narrative, facts are easily forgotten. A story broken down into its most basic form is built upon cause and effect.

Uri Hasson, a neuroscientist at Princeton, has conducted experiments using a functional magnetic resonance imaging (fMRI) machine to study the brains of both storytellers and listeners. The research finds that a story is the only way to activate parts of the brain so that a listener turns the story into their own ideas and experience. His conclusion from the research is that storytelling is the only way to successfully plant ideas into the minds of others.[1]

Storytelling makes sense as a way to infuse people with your company's expertise, ideas, and thoughts. As marketers, this is just what we want to have happen when buyers and customers engage with our digital content and communications. For, if we can get them to use our ideas as their own in discussions with their colleagues on the buying committee, our company is theoretically "in the room"—even if not physically.

But it's important to create a "real" narrative. If the story doesn't make sense to the listener, then this transfer of ideas and thoughts doesn't take place. This is yet one more reason why the driving force behind digital relevance is how well marketers know their buyers and customers and why the structure of the business stories they create is a critical element.

Also key in a story is the moment of change. Stories must show resolution of the trouble that started them and the achievement of the goal the hero went in search of. Movement is important—along with surprise—to keep the brain of the listener from being bored. How these elements are applied within the structure of the story is what makes them successful.

Stories inherently have a problem-to-solution structure. Most stories are about humans facing problems and trying to overcome them. Stories start with trouble. Whatever has gone wrong for the hero is the catalyst for the story, as well as what makes it gripping and interesting. If the hero was having a great day and everything was going her way, we wouldn't care. In fact, we'd be bored. This is because there would be no excitement, no surprise, no challenge, and no movement from the hero in trying to overcome obstacles to achieve a goal.

Other studies have found that brain networks used to interpret stories overlap with the networks used to navigate interactions with people where we're trying to figure out the thoughts and feelings of others.[2] In other words, your brain will react to immersive stories in the same way it would respond to having the fictional experience in real life.

The words also play a key role in your prospect's ability to become immersed in the story. Overused words, as well as words recognized as jargon, tend to lose their impact and be ignored. The studies found that a phrase such as "having a rough day" had become so overused that it failed to stimulate the brain. Take this as a case in point about why your content will become more relevant if you avoid the use of buzzwords.

Storytelling evokes a strong neurological response and has been used to change attitudes and behaviors for centuries. Neuroeconomist Paul Zak's research indicates that our brains produce the stress hormone cortisol during the tense moments in a story, which allows us to focus, as well as oxytocin, the feel-good chemical that promotes connection and empathy during the emotional moments of a story.

In one experiment after participants watched an emotionally charged movie about a father and son, Zak asked study participants to donate money to a stranger. With both oxytocin and cortisol in play, those who had the higher amounts of oxytocin were much more likely to give money to someone they'd never met.[3]

Suspension of Disbelief

Research in the field of neuroscience has offered some scientific basis for explaining the phenomenon of the "willing suspension of disbelief." Stories require a certain level of conscious decision to be open to something that you might otherwise be skeptical about. Suspension of disbelief happens when your audience becomes interested enough or emotionally invested enough to accept the story you're sharing as plausible. The research cited previously has found that the capability to actually sync your brain activity with that of the storyteller gives well-constructed, relevant stories more power to persuade.

Whether you realize it or not, as a marketer you are meant to be a storyteller. Marketers articulate the value of their company's products in a way that they believe will persuade a person to make a decision to buy. Your ability to convince your audience to suspend disbelief long enough for them to make your ideas their own is a key factor in your stories succeeding in doing this.

Think about the last time you watched a movie or read a novel and were totally enthralled in the story, rooting for the hero to prevail. At that moment in time, it was as if their world was your world. The actions of the characters and the twists and turns of the plot line seemed totally plausible and as if they were actually happening.

This is the quality of the story marketers will need to develop if they are to help their company's prospects and customers visualize a future in which their problem is solved with the help of your product or solution and expertise. The better you know your prospects and customers, the higher your probability for success in creating a willingness to suspend disbelief.

However, it's important to remember that sustained engagement will require that your story not take leaps of faith that your audience is not prepared to accept. If you push too hard or too fast, the result can be a break in this level of engagement because your audience will find your storyline implausible. Just because science has found a link in brain activity to help the audience invest in the experience as if it's their own doesn't mean an ill-constructed story will do the trick.

Conflict Is Compelling

Conflict is about pushback that creates tension and uncertainty. Change creates conflict, and conflict creates change. In a fictional story, conflict is whatever is keeping the hero or heroine from getting to happily ever after. In a business story, conflicts are the obstacles that keep the buyer from solving a problem or attaining an objective. Conflict is essential to the plot of your story. It creates the twists and turns that make the story compelling. In a business story, conflict is about mirroring the real-world dilemmas that get in the way of change that leads to buying and showing your prospects how to resolve the obstacles that arise at each stage of the buying process.

There will usually be more than one type of conflict in a business story unless what you are selling is a simple transaction. Conflict is one of the key elements of a story that drives momentum and interactions. This is because conflict is active. It acts against whatever your prospect is trying to achieve. As your prospect removes one conflict, another will appear. It's this process of working through the conflicts in the quest of resolving a problem that creates momentum. As the prospect gains competence at defeating conflicts, his confidence grows.

Conflict is compelling because it raises questions and doubts. Will the hero make it through? Conflict is also a sort of confrontation. Most people don't like confrontation, but are fascinated by others forced to deal with it. A simple example is the rubbernecking that occurs on the freeway after an accident, or the way people gather around a fight. Conflict in a business story will likely involve some type of disagreement, such as a lack of consensus, or a limitation, such as a lack of budget allocation or the fear associated with a perception of high risk.

Conflict becomes more compelling when your prospect has an investment in the outcome. If your product or company is positioned as the hero of the story, this investment will not happen because there will be no impact to the prospect or customer. It is only when the story is radically relevant to them that they are rooting for the hero to win—in essence, rooting for themselves. Seeing themselves in the hero is essential to their developing this level of vested interest.

In a business story, conflict used effectively will help create sustained engagement across the entirety of the buying process, for the story cannot reach a conclusion until all of the conflicts are resolved. Resolution in a business story is the decision to buy—hopefully from you. Resolution is the change in state from chaos to order.

Progressive Transformation

The hero of a story is not the same at the end of the story as she was at the beginning. At each stage of the story, the hero or buyer learns something necessary to allow her to overcome a conflict that would otherwise keep her from taking the next step. As a prospect traverses the stages of the buying process, transformation takes place.

One of the reasons that strategy is so important for digital marketers is that we must progress our stories in line with the evolution of our prospects. The prospect who is engaging in the story during the options stage of buying does not have the same mind-set and beliefs as the prospect in status quo who has yet to realize there's a better way.

By mapping stories and content to buying stages or customer lifecycle stages, marketers are better able to match story intent with buying intent. This also explains why content that works well at one stage of buying may produce lackluster results if used in another stage. It's the difference between cracking the spine of a book and turning to page one or randomly opening a chapter and beginning to read. Orientation is established in the first and overlooked in the second. Without the appropriate orientation, the comfort level won't be achieved that allows for suspension of disbelief or "buy-in" to the story.

In a digital marketing scenario, this is why it's key to "connect the dots" between content assets. This allows a prospect to easily gain the orientation they need to invest in the story being shared at a point that makes sense for them given the transformation they've already experienced along their journey. This is not something that happens by accident—not usually. It requires purposeful orchestration.

Although marketers don't often have their audience from start to finish, as a novelist or filmmaker does, the channels and story elements can be combined to engage prospects at whatever stage they are in when they find your story. Since research shows that the number of content assets buyers engage with during the buying process is growing—anywhere between 5 and 12, based on which research study you believe—there are many opportunities for the story that is shared to contribute value to a company's business objectives.

CHAPTER 14

The Strategic Value of Storytelling

S torytelling provides a solid foundation and consistency for digital marketing. The better you apply what you know about your prospects and customers, the more relevant your story will be. The nature of a business story construct with a continuum approach is that it's built to flex. It can be expanded and contracted as needed to deal with persona, industry, and marketplace changes. Storytelling is a long-term strategy that keeps companies from straying from their distinct value that matters to their customers. Done well, storytelling is representative of a company's "true north."

However, because companies base their progress on calendar goals, it's become commonplace to seek changes to strategy on an annual basis, sometimes sooner. Planning used to cover longer ranges of three to five years, but with the rapid pace of change, shifts to strategy are coming closer together.

The beginning of the year is when a lot of companies look at what they want to accomplish during the next annual period as a clean slate. This is often approached as if starting from scratch with an "out with the old, in with the new" type of mind-set.

A few drivers for corporate resets come to mind:

- Executives come up with new "themes" they want to see tackled.
- Company objectives may take a turn given market fluctuations or board consensus, or the CEO's new hyper interest.
- A new channel looks like a big opportunity for extending reach. Everyone's starting to jump on board, and you don't want to be left behind. But that means something will have to go to make room/ budget for it.

- Regulations shift, opening up a new market.
- Quotas go up.
- A new product is being introduced.
- And everyone's favorite: budgets get slashed!

Change has become the norm for businesses—and not just at the beginning of the year. But, unless your digital marketing strategy and programs were crap last year, taking a clean-slate approach is not the best response.

While you weren't looking, your buyers began expecting their experience with your brand's story to be a continuum. Not a jerky, stop and start, switch horses in mid-stride, confusing experience based on a new campaign each month or quarter.

This means your strategic storytelling approach is better off holding course. If it's been built around the distinct value your company provides to the specific markets you serve, it's primed to scale, shift, and morph without the need to start over. Room for adjustments is built in.

Before marketers shift course, they must determine why they're making choices. Just because your company is changing a few things doesn't mean your buyers' needs, objectives, preferences, and problems have changed. If you start making shifts to the story you're telling without considering the ramifications of alienating your audience, you could be tossing away more than one marketing approach for another.

Ask the following questions based on the internal changes you're reacting to with your annual strategic plan:

- Has something about your persona (buyers, customers) changed?
- Have the problems your personas are trying to solve changed?
- Has the way the industry is approaching these problems changed?

If the answer to any of those is "yes," then you have some work to do to realign the story you're telling. If the answer is "no" (which will be true in relation to most internal corporate changes), then the next step is to consider the change relative to your buyers and customers (markets).

- What parts of the internal changes will be visible to your markets and how are those changes relevant to them?
- Does this change invalidate anything you've said/done in the past that would create a fragmented experience for your markets? How can you adjust for this?

- In order to achieve this new objective, what really needs to change? Why? This could include things such as process, editorial calendars, talent, timing, and so on.
- Given your current marketing strategy, how can you holistically incorporate the change into your current strategy? Where does it fit the most seamlessly with what you're already doing?
- How will we measure, validate, and report on the impact from the change? And how could the change impact the metrics you're currently using to measure performance?

Digital marketing strategy must be designed as a continuous process that lives and breathes the brand story. As such, it has the flex to shift and be tweaked and refined, based on modifications to corporate objectives. Marketers need to think about how the change will shift the story in relation to what's most relevant to your markets.

With a continuum approach based on storytelling, changes can be incorporated in midstride. Storytelling enables marketers to adapt to changing company dynamics while retaining respect for their audiences. Maintaining consistency with the story you've been telling while adding new "chapters" to incorporate internal objectives or new product offerings will help pull your buyers along with those shifts without diminishing their engagement in the story. Even a corporate rebranding can be incorporated successfully within a story based on distinct value, personas, and a structure that allows the strategic approach to flex without breaking.

Storytelling Is a Process for Continuous Improvement

Digital marketing has the most opportunity for relevance that marketing has had at any other time in the past. The reason for this has a lot to do with the technology digital marketers rely upon. The data gathered from digital marketing programs, along with the analytics to make sense out of it, allows digital marketers to gain insights from their audiences as they introduce each new "scene" and "chapter" of the story. Whether through sentiment and sharing posted by your audiences via social channels, or insights gleaned from engagement and progression of prospects that is derived from the website, blog, and nurturing programs, marketers have the ability to respond to what they learn by refining the content employed. Improvements based on this data will help prospects engage more readily in the moment, resulting in their spending more time with your story.

Conversely, gleaning insights from marketing that is campaign driven is based on conducting a review after the end of the short-term program with a "what worked and what didn't" evaluation. Waiting until after the fact does not help engage prospects and customers in the moment. In fact, this could actually be costing you attention the longer an underperforming campaign stays in play. Real-time and responsiveness are key attributes enabled by storytelling that provides strategic value through enabling continuous improvements to performance.

A few reasons why continuous improvement is imperative include the following:

- Storytelling structure is based on extensions of the part of the story already shared. If you know that the part of the story you just shared engaged your prospects, building on that engagement with the next piece of the story becomes easier to achieve.
- Stories are progression machines. Each new addition to the story is designed to help those who engage with it make progress toward resolution, also known as buying.
- As your prospects ingest your ideas and vicariously live the experience of solving their problem with your help, your ideas influence their ideas. Stories can put your company in the room without a physical presence, influencing hallway discussions and buying committee meetings.

Proving performance as you go helps set benchmarks that marketers can continue to improve upon. The analytics and social sentiment will serve to validate the effectiveness of your storytelling, as well as provide near real-time insights for refinements along the way.

A continuum approach also allows marketers to use metrics in a fluid manner. What happens in one stage of the continuum will influence progress made in the next and so on. As momentum increases, cycle times will shorten. More buyers will make it throughout the process because bottlenecks can be identified and removed quickly. Salespeople will accept and pursue more of the leads that marketing generates because the quality will be noticeably higher. And salespeople will close more deals as they help buyers complete the story to achieve resolution.

No More Dr. Jekyll and Mr. Hyde

Digital marketing is obviously reliant on the Internet. The increasing use of channels that companies don't own means it's easier for marketers to lose control of their history. Something posted today on social media or a community forum or even a guest post on an industry blog could be around forever. If it's not aligned with your brand, it will remain there for all to see, potentially confusing your buyers and customers. But we tend to forget this and proceed as if the slate has indeed been wiped clean because we decide to change our story. Digital relevance requires a big picture view that encompasses internal as well as external impacts.

Just as your buyers experience progressive transformation, so must your digital marketing. This is achieved most gracefully as the evolution in story, not as the ending of one campaign to start a new one with a different focus. Because marketers don't often experience their marketing as their customers do—which they should—they are unaware that the whiplash their buyers experience at the other end can make their companies appear like Dr. Jekyll one day and Mr. Hyde the next. Conversely, sticking with storytelling alleviates this syndrome.

When I reviewed the first B2B Content Marketing Benchmarks, Budgets and Trends Report conducted by MarketingProfs and Junta42 (now CMI) back in 2010, it struck me that the challenges marketers face have remained eerily similar. This is a span of five years.

The top challenge in 2010 for 36 percent of marketers was producing *engaging* content, followed by producing *enough* content. In the 2014 report, 47 percent of marketers say that producing engaging content is a challenge (preceded by lack of time and producing enough content). Instead of getting better, the situation has gotten worse.[1]

This lack of progress is also reflected in the B2B Content Preferences Study of buyers conducted by DemandGen Report since 2011. Although buyer reliance on content during the buying process has grown from 47 percent in 2011 to 75 percent in 2014, the relevance of vendor content has declined across the board, with only 35 percent of buyers willing to consider vendor content as trustworthy in 2014. More buyers are now asking marketers to provide greater value, focus less on products, and use more data and research to back up their claims in 2014 than they have in the past.

Fifty-nine percent of buyers considered vendor websites relevant in 2013. Only 50.5 percent of buyers are willing to say so today. As more evidence, 65 percent of buyers found white papers relevant in 2013, which dropped to 53.4 percent in 2014. Webinars showed the biggest drop, from 65 percent of buyers finding them valuable in 2013, to only 42.6 percent finding them valuable in 2014.[2] Marketers, even with years of content marketing experience under their belts, are becoming less relevant to buyers. This trend needs to stop, and stop now.

Storytelling can help correct all of these issues, for marketers and for buyers.

Keith Quesenberry, a researcher at Johns Hopkins University, predicted that the Budweiser Puppy spot would be a winner during the 2014 Super Bowl after conducting a two-year analysis of 108 Super Bowl commercials. In a paper published in *The Journal of Marketing Theory and Practice,* Quesenberry and research partner Michael Coolsen focused on brands' use of specific strategies to sell products, such as featuring cute animals or sexy celebrities. But they also coded the commercials for plot development and story.

What they found, regardless of the content of the ad, is that the structure of the content predicted its success. Ads based on story structure were more engaging.[3] This really shouldn't be a surprise. Humans have been telling stories since they were written on the walls of caves.

CHAPTER 15

Story Structure—8 Elements of Story Design

Stories work because of their structure. The elements used to design a business story all work together to paint a relevant picture that encourages your audience to suspend disbelief while they engage with it. While the elements of story are universal, the way they are applied in business stories has a few variations.

Setting: In a novel or movie, the setting is the world built for the characters to explore, such as the fictional environment of the hospital in the TV series *Gray's Anatomy* or the asteroid on a direct path to destroy the world in the movie *Armageddon*. In a business story, setting is the context of your prospects' status quo situation. It can vary between industry verticals or in relation to the problem being addressed, as well as with the size of company that comprises your target audience.

Character: All stories need characters to play out the action and achieve the goal. We need someone to root for and someone or something to root against. In a business story, there are at least three characters: hero, villain, and mentor.

- The hero is your buyer or customer. They are the ones with a problem to solve or a goal to achieve. This is not negotiable.
- The villain is the problem that gets in the way of the goal or objective. Depending on the type of solution you sell, the villain can also be the options, other than your solution, for solving the problem. This doesn't necessarily mean competitors, although it could. It means options other

than choosing the type of solution you sell or choosing to do nothing. One example could be choosing to use manual tools, such as spreadsheets, rather than technology to automate a repetitive process. The villain, or antagonist, could also be a stakeholder who is a strong opponent of the solution and remains steadfastly against helping the hero achieve consensus. This last scenario will most likely play out during late-stage involvement of the hero and the buying committee with your sales team.

• The mentor is the person to whom the hero turns for the advice and knowledge they need to amass in order to overcome obstacles to achieve the goal. An obvious example is the Fairy Godmother in the children's story "Cinderella." Without the Fairy Godmother, Cinderella would never have made it to the ball or found her prince. In a business story, the mentor is you, your company. To be very clear, it is not your products, but your expertise and distinct value.

Plot: The plot is your storyline based on the route from problem to solution that is necessary for your buyer to navigate to gain the knowledge needed, as well as the confidence to achieve consensus for buying what you sell. The stages of the buying process provide the framework for story development, along with the questions your prospects need to have answered as they traverse each stage. Note that the plot is based on the element of theme and that each stage of progress along the plot line will include answering the small questions along the way that roll up under the theme represented by your persona's value proposition or big question.

Conflict: As discussed in chapter 13, conflict creates the tension that makes the story interesting. Conflict provides the pushback against your prospect making progress toward achieving the goal. It can be as simple as a stakeholder saying no, or as difficult as the need for a change management initiative that affects adjacent departments. Conflict consists of all the possible things that can happen to prevent your buyer from achieving his business objective. Note that conflict can be preexisting as the reason the goal hasn't been achieved in the first place. Risk also introduces conflict in a business story.

Climax: This is what I call a Step Back during the buying process. This is the final hurdle that must be overcome to keep your buyer moving forward to the purchase decision. It's whatever might lead to losing the deal. It could be something that's remained unaddressed and needs to be resolved in order for the buyer to proceed. Or it could be someone on the buying committee who stalls the process with a question that's not arisen previously. Climax is also referred to as the black moment in a story. It's the point in time when it appears all is lost. In a business story, this could be represented by a stall in forward momentum when the decision to buy seemed imminent. Often, it is caused by a person with authority who walks into the consensus meeting and asks, "What if...?"

Resolution: This is how you help the hero respond to whatever caused the Climax, in order to restore confidence in the buying committee to help them reach consensus. By removing perceived doubts and risks you enable your buyer to take the next step to validate you as his company's partner of choice...and buy.

Dialogue: This is the two-way communication you design to integrate your story elements in order to engage your prospects over the course of their buying process. Dialogue is not about you talking and them listening. It's about building an interactive relationship through how you design and use your content in the forums where your prospects spend their time, including on your website. A story is interactive. A monologue will not accomplish converting a prospect to a buyer.

Theme: This is your persona's value proposition, or big question, and the backbone of your story.

I need_____to help me to_____in order to_____.

An example could be, *I need a better way to help me build prospect engagement and progression in order to increase the quality of leads passed to the sales team.* In question format, it could be, *How can I build prospect engagement that increases the quality of sales-ready leads?* Sometimes questions are easier. Use what works for you. But notice that theme is not based on your company's value proposition, but your persona's. It must be your hero's story.

Incorporating these eight elements of story design into your strategic approach to digital marketing will increase your relevance maturity. The resulting narrative will engage prospects because it is grounded in their situation and aligned to their role and responsibility at the company where they work. Your talking about your products will bore them to tears. Your talking about the situations they're dealing with in a context they understand—one that helps them visualize solving their problem with your help—will hold their attention and help them transition across each stage of buying.

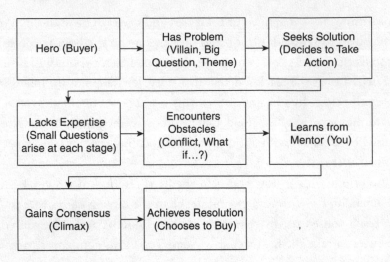

Figure 15.1 A Simple Structure for Story Design.

Story design can be as complex or as simple as you choose to make it. The figure above shows a simple structure visually to help you understand how the elements work together:

Helping Buyers Find Their Place in the Story

Each decision-maker, influencer, champion, or end user has a potentially different place in the story regarding how to solve the company's problem. This is one of the reasons that developing personas is so important. Content written for one persona has a diminished chance to thoughtfully engage the specific needs of others. Generic content has less chance of engaging anyone because it's not designed to speak with anyone.

We're all familiar with the acronym WIIFM? (What's in it for me?). For some reason, marketers haven't applied it to the content they develop for their digital marketing programs, or their relevance wouldn't be declining so rapidly.

For example,

- Will an end user care about ROI ratios?
- Will an IT developer care that the marketing department will need less head count once they have your system?
- Will the chief financial officer (CFO) care that the ease of use for end users will increase employee satisfaction and morale?

The likely answer to each of the above is, not really.

Unfortunately, marketing content is often written to address a whole kitchen sink full of benefits that apply so widely that no one can find their place in the story. But, when content is narrowly focused to provide clarity for a specific persona, it's so damn relevant that they can't ignore it. By allowing the persona to find their role in the story, they are able to see your solution or product from a new and immediately relevant angle. They can personally identify with the value that's just for them.

With this clarity, they can then visualize how your solution can be helpful to them. When they decide it's worthwhile to pursue, they'll start helping others figure out their places in the story. This is what happens when your prospects can ingest your ideas and make them their own, so much so that they're invested in sharing those ideas with others.

When your prospects find personalized value, pipeline momentum builds. Through them, your reach extends to others within the company that you haven't been able to engage on your own. With their place in the story clear, prospects become more active in taking the next steps toward solving the problem that's holding them or their companies back.

CHAPTER 16

Contextualization and Channel Integration

D igital marketing uses an ever-increasing number of channels. Each channel has a unique cadence and context that must be addressed to improve the relevance of marketing communications. Likewise, each persona that is engaged has a unique context. Becoming radically relevant is dependent on a marketer's ability to merge the context of the channel with the context of the buyer they're trying to engage and to reflect that in the content they share.

Context refers to the circumstances that surround a given situation and determine the meaning for whomever is involved. When circumstances are taken out of context, meaning can be misconstrued. However, just as importantly, the makeup of the person put in the circumstances of the situation will affect the meaning. For example, a finance executive may interpret a situation as fraught with risk, whereas an entrepreneur in the same situation sees massive opportunity. Perspective makes all the difference.

One of the difficulties marketers encounter, especially with social media, is how to engage more than one persona. If you have five personas to market to who all engage on Twitter, but your Tweets speak only to one or two of them, your marketing has less reach and is less effective overall.

The most common solution for this dilemma is to create numerous profiles, pages, or accounts on a platform, with each one meant to focus on different company initiatives (customer service or marketing) or industries (financial services, healthcare, technology), or product categories (mobile, cloud, big data). While this may make sense theoretically, the result is often more silos to manage and maintain—and more opportunities for your company's distinct value to get muddled. Depending on the quality of execution, the various accounts can also create fragmented stories that confuse prospects and customers.

Perhaps a better solution from a digital marketing perspective would be to focus a social media account on a problem-to-solution story line. Done this way, the thread of the dialogue within the profile is sharing one, cohesive story in which prospects engaged in solving the problem can find information relevant to them, as well as content relevant for others on the buying committee who need the information. Think of this as more of a community approach than an individual one. How well it's implemented could play a role in speeding time to consensus, as the idea is to involve all the stakeholders in the decision. Helping them understand differing points of view in relation to the problem and solution could help them see ways to help themselves and the others who are involved get what they want with your help.

Alternatives to separate profiles may be using tags or categories on a blog or in a forum, or hashtags on Twitter or discussion topics in LinkedIn groups. The point is to make sure that the story can be found by those to whom it's most relevant in relation to the context that can be identified.

Similarly, websites must present content within a context that buyers and customers will appreciate. Standard navigation is built on silos that make it difficult for your audience to know what to do in order to get what they want. The audience for a website is made up of a variety of people with a variety of interests and needs. Given the dependence on digital channels, it's becoming more difficult to present the right information to the right person at the right time. Technology, such as the platform offered by Demandbase, or web content management that includes tools to address context and personalization, such as CoreMedia (both are clients), can help marketers master the challenge. Another technology that is helping marketers address context is marketing automation. But the technology won't help if you don't have the strategy and the story to support the execution it makes possible.

Putting Channels in Context

Channels are often considered in isolation and in relation to their broadcast capabilities. As an example, Twitter is considered to be a channel based on immediacy. It has been suggested that the life of a Tweet ranges between 15 minutes and a few hours. Based on this belief, it's not uncommon to see marketers tweeting out the same message three or four times per day. Unfortunately, they choose to do this in the most unimaginative way possible, by using the title and link in every posting—in other words, repeating the same Tweet at different times throughout the day or week. The goal is not relevance as much as it is a quest to broadcast the message in search of more clicks and shares. One only needs to look at the account's profile page to see the list of repetitive Tweets.

LinkedIn discussion groups are based on the idea of collaboration and networking with professionals interested in similar topics. Unfortunately, the groups have become a dumping ground for marketing promotions that may include a couple of sentences in addition to the title and link, but it's usually obvious that there's no real intention to "discuss" the topic. This is made obvious through the many discussions in which members of the group have posted comments in relation to the posts, but the marketer who started the discussion has never returned to answer or interact. While group administrators try to maintain order and the integrity of discussions, marketers still do their best to broadcast and pull traffic back to their sites without consideration for the context of the channel or the purpose of a discussion group.

Influencers within industries can also be construed as a channel, a replacement for seeking media placement with traditional publishers. Unfortunately, the approach marketers take is akin to pushing press releases to journalists, and about as successful. What's changed is that influencers don't have a quota to fill. They don't need to publish a certain number of stories each day. What's missing most in the way marketers pursue influencers about sharing their content and stories is that the context of the influencer is not usually considered. No relationship is built ahead of time to pave the way. Emails are sent with press releases asking for coverage, without consideration to why the information may be relevant to the influencer. In essence, this is an attempt to hijack an audience carefully built by the influencer without respect for the influencer.

The thing to note here is that influencers don't owe marketers anything. Their responsibility is to their audience and meeting their expectations, delivering on the promise that keeps them coming back. Posting a press release or taking the time to craft it into a compelling story is an imposition on the influencer's time. However, with the right approach and groundwork, influencers can be swayed. Once again, it's about relevance.

Taking the time to show respect for the influencer by leaving meaningful comments on their blog and sharing their content can go a long way toward breaking the ice to engage them when the time comes. Just as with your prospects, you are not the only one seeking their attention and participation.

Each channel that marketers put in use will have different requirements and expectations by those who frequent it. It's imperative that marketers not only learn the nuances of the channels they incorporate into their digital programs, but that they develop a plan for interactivity that integrates with the story they're sharing.

The Need for Channel Integration

Digital marketers should think of channel integration as the equivalent of a business treasure hunt. Each content asset presented within a channel is an informational clue to a part of the story about the problem-to-solution journey for the hero. Channel integration is successful when it "connects the dots" for the hero and invites further engagement in the story.

Channel integration is answering the question, what do you want them to do next?

It's imperative for marketers to understand how a part of the story shared in one channel can be extended with a part of the story shared in another, and so on. This means that you need to know how your content assets fit together in relation to the problem-to-solution story for each persona.

Here's a simple example to consider:

- You post a Tweet that links to a blog post.
- The blog post includes an offer for an eBook.
- The eBook includes a link to a video.
- The video includes a link to an article at the end.
- The article includes an invitation to a webinar on the subject.
- The webinar includes follow-up with a workbook.
- The workbook invites the audience to participate in a discussion group on LinkedIn that is created for that specific purpose.
- After a vibrant discussion on LinkedIn, the prospect sends InMail to one of your salespeople who engaged them by answering their questions or providing a new idea for consideration.

All of the content used in the above example is related to the problem your buyer is trying to solve. It's been well thought out, structured into a business story that builds momentum through increased engagement, and distributed purposefully in channels the persona is known to use. Even if the prospect were to step into the story in midstream, she would have the ability to engage in the story and keep moving. There are also opportunities within some of the content to provide links both backward and forward to allow choice based on the prospect's buying stage.

Channel integration requires considerations of story, format, progression, and interactive dialogue. Miss any of these and your channels could become dead ends. After all, it's great if your content garners a lot of views. It's better if it leads to the next step to extend engagement, and your prospects take you up on the offer.

PART 2

Dynamic Execution—Put Strategy in Play

To execute on the strategy created in Part 1, marketing skills need to be transformed and perspectives need to change. Based on your company's distinct value, personas, and story lines, execution must be swift, continuous, on-target, and quantifiable against contribution to revenues. Many marketing professionals are finding that their compensation now depends on accountability to revenue performance. This is challenging to address, as many companies haven't changed the way that overall marketing programs are measured. Marketers often feel that they lack visibility to data and deal progression once sales takes over the conversation with a prospect who has reached the opportunity stage.

Marketers will find more confidence if their visibility and participation are extended across the entire buying cycle with a continuum-style of execution. They'll also understand and begin to appreciate the value of staying involved throughout the buying process by helping salespeople become more valuable to prospects. Because they'll be able to track prospect behavior even after sales becomes involved, they'll have a better understanding about what it takes to go from a sales opportunity to gaining a new customer. The possibility for a true partnership between marketing and sales presents a huge opportunity for sustainable competitive advantage.

The basis for real-time marketing is responsiveness. But not just any response will do. There's an art and a science to creating the agility necessary to communicate across channels and platforms with varying orientations, as well as with stakeholders who hold differing perspectives. One-size-fits-all marketing will not get the job done. Applying context to responsiveness is a critical skill necessary for attaining radical relevance.

In this part of the book, I present marketers with the insights, skills, and tools they need to add true value to the buying process during execution. They'll gain capabilities needed to elevate their companies to credible and trusted experts that buyers and customers come to rely upon to reach professional and personal success.

Not only will marketers learn how to execute in a way that accelerates goal achievement but they'll also be armed with the ability to educate their executive team about how they contribute to business objectives with the metrics to prove it.

SECTION 5

Responsiveness—Your Ability to Sync Up

B uyers and customers expect companies to be responsive. They know companies are watching them, yet the lack of action that companies take in response to buyer and customer behavior remains frighteningly low. If you watch brands online, it often appears that they're oblivious to what's going on around them as they continue to push product messages and promote themselves. In this section, marketers will learn how to listen in order to understand how to respond. They'll see how their responsiveness translates to the relevance maturity matrix and how the two competencies work together to increase their mastery of digital marketing on a real-time basis.

Responsiveness means the ability to readily react to suggestions, influences, behavior, and dialogue with prospects and customers externally; and with salespeople, product managers, customer service, and the executive team internally. Being responsive requires critical thinking if it is to be executed purposefully as a driver of improved performance.

As is true with relevance, responsiveness is achieved in stages. Taking an iterative approach to responsiveness will help marketers adapt. Becoming a responsive marketing organization is a change for most companies. Marketers will find it easier to adapt as they learn new skills along the way. Responsiveness stages align fairly closely with relevance maturity. Progress made in both competencies will deliver payoffs that help marketing forever eradicate the "fluff" designation. Given the expanded role digital marketing plays, it's imperative for marketing teams to become a respected and crucial asset to the company based on a tangible contribution to business imperatives.

The Conundrum of Choice

While marketers plan out their content strategies and map content to buying stages, they must also realize that strategy is a starting point. The secret to becoming truly relevant relies on what happens when you take the strategy to market, in addition to your ability to be flexible and agile in response to its reception in the marketplace.

One of the biggest complaints I hear from marketers is that content doesn't necessarily result in prospects' choosing to "do" something that indicates increased engagement or intent to take a next step toward purchase. Most of the time this lack of action on the prospect's part is because the choice of what to do next isn't obvious or doesn't exist. Or, if it is present, the choices are not relevant, given how the buyer or customer interpreted the content they just viewed based on their stage in the buying process. When either of these situations is true, your audience either clicks around online trying to find something that extends the dialogue they embarked upon, or they move on.

The problems I see are caused by the way marketers have aligned content to buying stages. Rather than introducing flexibility that more than one choice can exist, they've ended up trying to dictate what's next by offering content that they think is a logical and linear progression. However, they often make this decision without actually knowing what stage a buyer is in or what they already may have learned to date.

Marketers remain under the illusion that they control the informational exchange. This is a big misconception. In an informational environment now driven by availability and choice, why do marketers think that limiting choice is the way to go?

I understand that marketers have budgets and that developing content has its limits, but marketers need to make thoughtful decisions about which options will be the most meaningful to their audiences. It's also crucial to consider what the options marketers choose to present can tell them about their buyers and customers as they interact with the content. It's not enough to know that they "clicked" or "viewed" a content asset. To be responsive, marketers must be able to gain insights from the context and information that was viewed.

There are a variety of ways in which choice can manifest those insights. Here are two examples.

Option 1:

- Prospect engages with an article on a web page.
- The "see also" sidebar options include links to a video, a webinar, and an infographic that extend the topic of the article.

Offering choices based on format can help you discern which type of content the prospect prefers and how much more time and attention they are willing to invest, should all three options be similar versions of the next part of the story. Sometimes it's the format that matters.

If this prospect only looks at infographics, then how serious are they about learning what they need to know to buy? Most infographics are lightweight data presentations that lack context and depth. Research has shown that infographics are also used most at the early stages of buying when prospects are unaware of the problem or working to understand the problem.[1]

However, if this prospect registers for a webinar on the same topic a few months later and attends, the behavior can tell you something quite different based on the amount of time they're willing to invest in learning more. Another insight that can be useful is to note what the formats tell you about the learning preferences of your audience. If you can identify patterns of engagement by stage, account, or persona, whether they are related to visual, audio, or written content, this data can be useful in your content development plans. Just make sure that you have a weighted sample to ensure that the choice made is responsive, and not reactionary.

Option 2:

- Prospect engages with a blog post.
- The hyperlinks in the text of the blog post offer three different perspectives related to the topic in the post. All of the links are to articles displayed on web pages, which removes the format as a factor in selection,

In this case, the link the prospect clicks on can provide insights into their view on the topic, perhaps even the persona with which they most closely align, and even the context of the problem they are working to solve.

If the person clicks on more than one link, this could indicate they have a higher urgency for learning more about how to solve the problem or meet the objective that's the focus of the content. However, clicking on more than one link can also mean they are looking for the content that most closely matches their context. Take a look at the time spent on the page. If the person spends 30 seconds on one article, but longer than three minutes on the second, then you have a basis for useful insight about which content mattered more to them.

It may seem like allowing buyers to "choose their own adventures" is a lot of work, but what you can learn by analyzing their choices can become input to improve the way your content addresses the buying process across stages. Offering more options can also result in speeding up the learning process, and hence the decision cycle. If your goal is building higher engagement with buyers, letting them lead the way through how they use your content can be transformative to your marketing performance. Assessing content with which prospects and customers choose to engage will help you make wiser choices about execution in the moments that count most—when you've got their attention.

Syncing Up

Syncing up is about aligning your content and marketing execution with each buyer's needs and preferences. The challenge for marketers is that traditional marketing has been a one-to-many exercise. Digital marketing has made it possible to narrow our focus to segments and even to 1:1 interactions in specific channels. The effort is not small. But effectiveness is directly related to the relevance of each and every interaction your company has with prospects and customers.

Responsiveness is a journey that will be accomplished in parallel with the development of relevance maturity. This section analyzes the four stages of responsiveness, including reactive, proactive, predictive, and dynamic. In each stage, marketers will be provided with insights into the skills and tools needed to manage the transition forward.

CHAPTER 17

The Reactive State

In the reactive state of digital marketing, responsiveness comes after the fact. Marketers wait for something to happen so that they can respond. One example is waiting for a form to be submitted so that a contact can be put into a nurturing program, or worse, sent to the sales team as a lead. Another is only engaging on social media when someone engages with your profile first. Rather than leading, marketers in a reactive state are following.

A reactive marketing organization will find its normal environment filled with chaos. Execution is more like firefighting with programs pushed out the door based on a timeline, rather than an approach to strategic engagement. A reactive marketing organization finds itself executing spur-of-the-moment campaigns based on an executive's idea of what would be cool to do, not necessarily because it's something prospects or customers will care about.

A Day in the Life of a Reactive Marketer

Diane sips her latte as she makes her way through Cloud Widget's maze of hallways to the three cubicles and bullpen of four desks that are her demand generation team's domain. She nods to Scott, their star salesperson, as she skirts him to take the file that Patty in public relations (PR) holds out as Diane passes her desk.

In her office, she deposits her briefcase next to her desk, surveying a couple of Post-its® that have been stuck to her desk blotter. Absently, she notices that the ivy plant on the windowsill could use some water. Taking her seat, she reads the first note:

Diane—Please create a new brochure for Widget X
Need it tomorrow for a meeting. Thanks, Scott

No wonder he didn't make eye contact when I passed him on my way in. What meeting? With whom and for what? As these questions run through Diane's mind, she peels off the second note:

Diane_I need to see the graphics for our virtual booth at TechSummit by tomorrow. We've decided to change the focus to Product B. Please make the adjustments. —Jerry

What does he mean, changing focus? Gail's been working on the graphics since last week. Ugh. Diane can feel her stress level rising, and she's only been in the office for ten minutes. It's going to be one of those days.

Taking another sip of coffee, she flips open the file Patty handed her and sees a press release about Widget X for TechSummit. At least I'm not the last one to know, she thinks as she considers all the other things for the booth that will need to be altered. Scanning the press release, she sees the requisite list of product features and the promotional discount offer. The suggestions she'd made about focusing on the customer had obviously been ignored.

At a knock on her door, she looks up and smiles at Susan, her social media whiz kid. "What's up?"

"Hey, boss. We've got a bit of an issue. The blog post that Jerry published making a direct comparison between Product B and Jacko's solution has received a pretty aggressive comment from a guy that appears to work at Jacko. And an analyst at Symbad wrote a blog post discrediting some of the points Jerry made in his post. Not directly, but it's being picked up on Twitter with links to both posts."

"Tell me you're kidding."
Susan crosses her arms and leans on the door jam.
"Okay, send me the links."
"In your inbox. Let me know what you'd like to do."

As Susan retreats to her desk in the bullpen, Diane leans back in her chair and sips her coffee, considering what to tackle first. She grabs a pad and makes a priority list.

- handle the social media issue
- check with Jerry about whether this changes his focus for TechSummit—again.
- update Patty on TechSummit—since no one else has
- call Scott to find out what he wants the brochure to highlight
- get Gail in graphic design to start working on the layout—and change the TechSummit graphics
- plus all the stuff on today's calendar…

While reviewing the comment made on Jerry's blog post and the post the Symbad analyst wrote, Outlook pops up a calendar reminder that her weekly agency call is starting in 15 minutes. She clicks snooze and grabs the phone to call Jerry.

"Hey, Jerry, this is Diane. Have you seen the comment on your blog post?"

"Yep. Those jerks are always trying to steal the limelight. I'm drafting a rebuttal."

Diane can feel the confrontational attitude coming through the phone. Jerry isn't the calmest of guys. He runs off adrenaline most of the time, which is usually helpful for a product category manager, but not in this situation. "What if I draft it for you? I think we need to defuse the situation. Nothing he said was that bad."

Jerry sputters. "Not that bad? He outright called me a liar!"

"No, he didn't. He challenged your point about business impact by asking for proof. We've got it, right?"

"Well, sure," Jerry pauses. "Anecdotally."

Diane lets go of the breath she didn't realize she was holding. "The next call on my agenda is to Scott. Why don't I ask if he can get a customer to speak up on our behalf?"

"That's a good idea. See if you can get a case study, while you're at it."

Diane forces herself not to react to the last part. Does he have any idea what that takes? She changes the subject. "By the way, does this put the focus for TechSummit back to Widget X?"

"Depends on whether Scott comes through. But with a customer testimonial, we've got an even better reason to stick with Product B. You've got the campaign set to launch the day after the summit, right? I want that discount offer to get a lot of traction. Sales is grouching about not having enough qualified leads."

Diane squeezes her eyes shut in frustration. "The campaign we prepared was for Widget X, so I'll need to rethink it. I'm not sure Gail has the bandwidth to create new graphics for all of this on such a short timeline, but I'll see what I can do. And, Jerry? Please don't post a response on the blog until I get back to you."

With Jerry calmed down, Diane clicks snooze again when the five-minute reminder for her meeting with the agency pops up, and she dials Scott's extension.

Calming the Chaos

Some version of the above "day in the life" scenario is the norm for companies in the reactive state of digital marketing. Marketing programs are compartmentalized and guided more by intuition and whim than by strategy. The focus is inside-out and product driven. In the reactive state, emotions and ego can cloud judgment because there's a lot of personal investment in each activity with nothing to align and balance them against the brand's story. While many reactive companies think they're beyond this stage because they've added new channels and tactics to the mix, it's easy to overlook their failure to raise relevance because they haven't changed how they think about and approach their prospects and customers.

Marketers who begin to listen to the marketplace their company serves will find the activity to be an important catalyst for moving away from the reactive state. Although you may think that listening will just fuel the flames of reactionary thinking, the opposite will become true. When listening broadens beyond your brand to the marketplace, the bigger picture becomes visible and allows for events, interactions, and commentary to be put into a contextual perspective.

Susan, who is on Diane's team, is listening. She's assessing the volume level of the reaction to Jerry's post along with the sentiment expressed. Susan is making sure that Diane knows what's going on in external channels. And, instead of reacting, she's alerted Diane and forwarded her the links to get her boss up to speed and seek input. What might elevate Susan's responsiveness is not limiting her action to being the messenger, but also having her bring ideas about next actions.

When putting together a response action plan related to a specific event, it's important to ask the following questions:

- What happened?
- What is the potential damage that's been done?
- What activity is it causing across channels?
- How might it affect brand perception?
- What are the different ways we could respond?
- What are the potential reactions by our audiences to those responses?
- What do we want our audiences to take away from our response?
- Which channels do we need to address?
- Whom do we need to advise internally about our response?
- What's the right thing to do?

By tackling the issue in a thoughtful way, companies in the reactive state can also gain multichannel comprehension. While it's important to address an issue in the channel where it was raised, as well as respond to the individual who raised it, creating a response action plan invites marketers to look beyond the original event.

Perhaps there's an opportunity to introduce a new dialogue about a facet of the issue that can invite positive engagement. Doing so would allow the company to take the lead in the conversation, rather than being reactionary. The requirement is to understand very clearly the sentiment of your audience in regards to the issue or topic at hand that enables the initiation of a thoughtful and meaningful dialogue. By taking an offensive rather than a defensive stance, a company can begin to move away from the reactive state.

CHAPTER 18

The Proactive State

The proactive state of marketing is demonstrated by marketers becoming more forward leaning and customer aware. Responsiveness is viewed by marketers as the opportunity to invite engagement and incite dialogue that speaks to more than products by sharing expertise. In this state, marketers recognize that being viewed as credible means adding value that's useful to addressing the problem or objective that may be top of mind for an audience.

Marketing may be ahead of the rest of the company in terms of understanding the audiences the company is trying to attract, engage, and persuade to buy what it sells—solutions to problems. The marketing team has been able to convince some of the leadership in the company of the value of a customer-driven content marketing approach. This is a continuous initiative to reinforce a customer-first mind-set and help colleagues form the habit of talking about what their products and solutions enable, rather than the features they include.

Progress is being made. Each small win earns marketers more investment in the concept and the commitment to the time needed to enact a longer-term view. Strategy, while still driven by the short term, is at least being documented, and planning is seen as a more formalized process. This doesn't mean that chaos has been totally eradicated, or that short-term whims won't creep in, but they are not a daily occurrence.

Channels are now being approached as opportunities with potential business impact, not just as places where the company needs to broadcast because its competitors have put a stake in the ground on that digital real estate. And marketers are also gaining access to modern technology platforms that will help them manage marketing programs and communications with prospects and customers, including marketing automation, social listening applications, and analytics.

A Day in the Life of a Proactive Marketer

Diane walks into the weekly Cloud Widgets demand generation team meeting carrying a box of Krispy Kreme donuts to the delight of everyone but Patty. She slides a yogurt parfait in front of the chronic dieter, smiling at her surprised delight. Once the others have helped themselves to the donuts, she snags the last maple bar, takes her seat at the table and gets down to business. "Okay, let's start with reviews. Susan, you're up first."

Susan plugs a thumb drive into the laptop hooked up to the projector and puts a slide of the company's social media activity up on the screen. "We had a pretty good week. Our LinkedIn group is up 12 members this week, putting the total at 189. The group posted five new discussions, which earned a total of 17 contributed comments. A pretty healthy discussion went on about chargeback methods for cloud applications. Perhaps that's a potential content opportunity."

Advancing to the next slide, Susan continues, "Our Twitter profile gained 27 new followers and lost 3. We posted 15 Tweets last week and had 8 Retweets. Our username was mentioned 42 times in relation to people tweeting our blog posts. The use of the #cloudrocks hashtag is picking up steam. I saw it used five times in relation to posts that weren't even ours."

Alan wipes his hands on a napkin. "Do we want that?"

Diane switches her focus from the screen to her analytics team member and says, "Yes. That's exactly what we want."

Alan looks confused. "Why? We created that hashtag to promote our stuff. What if competitors, namely Jacko, start using it to promote their stuff? I can't wait to hear what Jerry has to say about that."

Diane tamps down her irritation at a few snickers around the table. "The idea is to create a community of like-minded people on Twitter. We want people to use the hashtag. The more people who follow it, the bigger an audience we'll have when we do post our content, even if they're not following our profile." A few members of the team nod in agreement.

"I don't know about that," Alan says. "How do we know that they'll be the right people?"

"How do you know they won't be?" Susan chimes in. "It's a public platform. Anyone can follow anyone or post whatever they want. With more exposure, we can cast a wider net, gain a bigger opportunity to attract people interested in the topics we're talking about."

Alan crosses his arms, preparing to dig in for a discussion. "The analytics are going to be skewed."

"Alan, why don't you pull together an example of what you mean, and we'll take a look at it next week. I'd also like to see what insights we can glean about the others who are using the hashtag and what content they're promoting." Alan nods, looking somewhat appeased, but Diane knows he'll be prepared to argue his case next week. She hopes that he'll find something in the analysis that proves her point. She makes a note to send him the white paper on community development that she received from Symbad Research last week.

"Okay, let's move on," Diane says, glancing at her watch. We need to stay on track. Is there anything else, Susan?"

"The blog is coming along, but the posts I'm getting from Jerry are still so product focused. He's not thrilled with some of my edits and changes them back."

"I'll speak to him." Diane makes a note on her tablet. "Mike, you're up."

Mike picks up his iPad and swipes to his notes. "The drip programs are doing okay, but our click-to-open ratios need some help. Our bounce and unsubscribe rates are down, so that's good." Mike scrolls down his notes. "While the time spent per page is improving, we're still not getting the multipage engagement that we'd hoped for." Mike clears his throat and glances at Diane. "I know you're not a big fan, but I found a list I'd like to buy to bulk up our database. The price is good, and the list is specifically IT directors and VPs."

"How many new leads did our eBook generate since we launched it last week?" Buying leads was not high on Diane's to-do list, but Scott has been asking for more leads for his sales reps, so maybe she'd have to consider it. This organic approach was taking more time than she'd hoped.

"Fifty-seven forms were completed, 10 of them with bad data. I sent the 47 I scrubbed over to Scott's team."

Mike shrugs when Diane raises her eyebrows and shakes her head.

"Hey, he asked for them. What did you want me to do?"

"I would have preferred if you'd told him to come and talk to me. Filling out a form is not the definition of a lead. Have you gotten feedback from the sales team?"

"A little. To your point, they don't seem very happy with them."

"I'll talk to Scott." Diane taps her fingers on the table, considering the list option. "Send me the information about the list, and I'll take a look. Do you have any ideas from the engagement metrics why people aren't clicking on the calls to action?"

Mike shrugs. "Maybe we should switch out the content offers and see if that helps."

"Can you come up with some suggestions by next week's meeting?"

"Will do," Mike says.

Diane shifts her attention to Patty. "How's the press release coming for our new client announcement?"

"DynaTech is a dream. And Jerry is all hopped up that they took a stab at Jacko in their testimonial." Patty pumps her fist in the air, and several members of the team laugh. "The bad news is that Krypto's legal team is a nightmare. I'm having a heck of a time getting sign-off on their executive's testimonial. As of yesterday afternoon, they don't want us to use their name or logo." Patty shakes her head. "I've got a call with their legal team later this afternoon. I'll share the DynaTech testimonial with them and maybe that will help."

"I bet Jerry isn't happy about that," Mike says.

Diane knows he won't be. "Patty, do the best you can. The word from above is to get the press release out before Jacko announces their product upgrades next week." Diane makes a note and crosses an agenda item off her list. "Let's talk about our Q2 white paper. Who's got thoughts on a topic idea?" Susan puts the slide featuring their chief information officer (CIO) persona up on the screen.

Pivoting to Proactive

Making the pivot from reactive to proactive is done in increments. In this scenario, Diane's team has made some solid progress. They're trying to build a community around a topic on Twitter, and drip marketing campaigns are underway with a focus on increasing engagement. While they are getting closer to customer first, they are still working with an operational mind-set based on what the company wants and what its competitors are doing, more so than what the customer wants. The struggle to take a longer-term view is evident in Mike's request to buy a list, rather than to build their database organically through better content and interaction design. It's also represented by Alan's pushing back on the idea that competitors might take up the use of the hashtag #cloudrocks and the lingering belief that the company can control the conversation in social media.

In the proactive stage, it's an imperative to learn to think holistically and commit to the time required to build customer-centric engagement. Building relationships rather than capturing contact information in form completions and labeling them leads must take precedence. Diane's team also needs to get on the same page about the personas they want to engage and their capability to engage them. Over the last three years, I've built more than 90 personas. Only a few have represented CIOs, mostly due to the size of the company those clients serve.

One of the reasons for this is that C-level executives tend to rely on their teams that have the most expertise in the problem being solved to do research and evaluation. They simply don't have the time. While the C-level may make the final decision or authorize the budget, the marketing team must truly ascertain whether or not they have the opportunity to reach and engage them based on the strategic value of the products they sell.

The exercise of building personas as active tools will help marketing teams grasp the bigger picture about how the stakeholders involved in making a buying decision interact and what those interactions taken as a whole signify. Understanding the dynamics of a buying committee can also be useful in developing a strategy that helps build ongoing relationships with those people, rather than focusing on transactional metrics, such as time spent on page as an averaging metric for overall response. Likewise, the focus on a white paper as a stand-alone content asset rather than as an integrated part of the story being shared shows a need for improvement in the team's approach.

The proactive state is related to Shifting Relevance on the RMM. Some of what marketing teams are doing is highly relevant, but the tendency to slip back into inside-out habits dies hard. In this state, not only must we be ruthless editors of the content we produce but also ruthless editors of our thinking. Pivoting to proactive is about continuing to move toward customer obsession. Marketers and the companies they work for may slip back into reactive mode—and that's okay. The trick is to recognize when it happens and turn it around faster. The ability to step outside of transactions to see the bigger picture will help proactive marketers continue to improve their relevance maturity. The path to Radical Relevance is one involving practice, determination, and continuous improvement.

CHAPTER 19

The Perceptive State

The perceptive state is about gaining insights that enable marketers to have a deeper understanding about what prospects care about based on how they engage and respond to marketing content and communications. Digital marketing is faster and more complex than traditional marketing. Conversations that marketing teams hold about data are no longer limited by application to traditional metrics, such as clicks, opens, and views in relation to a campaign or the website or blog. Perceptive marketers reach much further toward a continuum approach in which one interaction begets another—adopting a cause-and-effect perspective.

Marketing teams in the perceptive state have taken context into account. They have become adept at identifying patterns of behavior indicative of a change in the propensity to buy. They have also developed conversational competence, allowing them to create more effective content marketing and social interactions in response to the current behavior they observe in digital channels. Due to a focus on continuous improvement, marketers in the perceptive state are better able to sustain engagement in the moment, as well as over time.

Collaboration and improved communications now take place regularly across all the functional roles of marketing. In the perceptive state, there is an attempt to remove the walls between the silos that were erected between marketing teams to make sure that one team knows what another is doing and that they can effectively support one another in strategic execution.

Collaboration is based on workflows, and is a more formalized process in comparison to the ad hoc methods that are prominent in the proactive state.

It is normal for the demand generation team to include the social media team in program and content planning, and for the social media team to request content from the demand generation team, for example. The social media team is also aware of what PR is doing and interfaces with the data analytics team to measure progress against goals and to monitor sentiment on relevant topics and the brand.

This marketing team has also reached proficiency with technology that enables them to take action more quickly than they were able to in the proactive stage. The team likely includes people with competence in the operation of marketing technology, enabling more of a "hands-on" approach to the execution of marketing programs, rather than waiting in a queue to deploy programs. They possess the ability to tweak and refine their programs on the fly because the ability to diagnose missteps has improved.

Drip marketing programs have become full-bodied, persona-based nurturing programs, and the quality of the leads sent to sales teams has improved dramatically. Rather than attempting to stay "top of mind" with a drip program, the demand generation team has discovered the power of sharing a progressive story line with a segment of prospects that align with a persona. With greater visibility into the behaviors of prospects and customers, the marketing team has reached the social relevance stage of maturity on the RMM.

A Day in the Life of a Perceptive Marketer

Putting the finishing touches on an email, Diane answers the phone, holding it between her ear and shoulder as she types.

"Hi, Diane, this is Scott. I just came out of an executive briefing, and my sales team needs to be selling the integration between Widget X and the Skylark SaaS collaboration platform by next quarter. We've got to start a customer education program, and my team is going to need tools and support. The quota we have to deliver based on new customer acquisition is…umm…aggressive. To have any chance of making it, we'll need for your team to get some lead gen offers out the door quickly."

"Okay, Scott. We'll get on it. Let me get my team up to speed, and then we should set aside some time for our teams to meet together next week."

Diane pulls up her team calendar and miraculously finds a half-hour open for all of them later in the day. She reserves a conference room and sends out the invitations for an all-hands meeting. A few years ago, Scott's request would have created chaos for her team based on its magnitude. She was proud that they were now able to take such requests in stride. While not ideal, these fire drills weren't happening nearly as often as they used to.

Later that afternoon, she walks into the conference room and notes that all the marketing teams are represented. "Thanks for making the time on such short notice. Let's get right to it since we only have 30 minutes." Diane takes her seat halfway down the middle of the long table and props her tablet in front of her. "Now that the merger with Skylark is complete and the developers have finished the integration with Widget X, the executive team wants to hit the ground running to gain market share by the end of the year. We need to have a full slate of programs in action by the start of Q3."

"But that's only a little more than one month away," says Patty. "I can't possibly get media placement that fast."

"Yes, you can," said Susan. "I've got some favors to call in for a few promotions and shares I've done in social media channels for some of your media contacts and the industry portals over the last few months. And I've built some good relationships with a couple of the industry influencers, so we should be able to get some earned media coverage, as well."

"Good. You two get together after the meeting and brainstorm some ideas." Diane loves it when her instincts about people pay off. Susan has made huge progress with their social media channels. "Now, let's map the changes and impacts for our personas. Who wants to start?"

Alan walks to the end of the table and hooks his laptop up to the projector. "I've been doing some monitoring across channels to learn more about how the integration might be perceived in the market." He puts a graph up on the screen. "The combination of the Widget X application development platform and the Skylark collaboration platform will help companies create an in-house application store for business users. It's kind of like an automation of the agile development process that enables service delivery on steroids."

The team groans and ribs Alan about his assessment.

"Wait. So our buyer is different?" Mike asks. "I've been reviewing our database and lead scoring process trying to figure out what might define segmentation for this new push and how the website and nurturing programs will need to be adjusted. I'd thought we could modify our story in line, rather than create a new one, but now I'm not so sure. We've got to engage with operations now."

"This integration doesn't negate the personas we've been engaging with, it adds a new one," Diane says. "But I'm not sure it's operations. Have we looked at the service delivery role? What about applications managers?"

"It would be useful if we had some customers using the platform," Mike says.

Diane picks up the phone and dials Jerry's extension. "Jerry? This is Diane. I'm in a meeting with the team to work on the expedited schedule for the launch. I'm putting you on speaker. We've got some customers testing the new Skylark integration in the field, right?"

"Yes. Lyhand Direct and Heller Services are both using it. I'm not sure how far along they are..."

"That's okay. What we need is to know who else came into the decision to use it. Do you think you can get the account guys to talk to Mike?"

"Sure. Mike, I'll send an introduction to you with their contact info and copy them."

"Thanks. That would be great," Mike says.

"We pushed all the Skylark documentation, brand documents, and content into a new section in the intranet. I'll set up access for your team, Diane. When do you think you'll have a draft of the marketing plan for me?" Jerry asks.

At least there is an air of humor in Jerry's question today. A year or so ago, he would have given her some ridiculous timeline. "Keep your socks on, Jerry," Diane laughs. "We just found out about this a couple of hours ago." She glances at her team. It looks like each of them is making a to-do list. Not one "deer in the headlights" look among them. "Maybe as soon as next week, Jerry."

Using Perceptions to Prosper

In the perceptive state, the marketing team is on the same page. They've recognized that their efforts contribute collectively to achieving business objectives their executives care about. The team has become proficient with technology and takes advantage of the functionality to push boundaries, including lead scoring. The difference in Diane's team is evident in the way they approach new marketing programs. Rather than reinventing the wheel for a new product launch, Mike's approach was to look at the story they were already sharing to identify opportunities to insert the new product into the "plotline."

When Alan presented his research into the market, the team instantly honed in on the need for a new persona. Before they begin talking about content and programs, they know they need to determine how the buying process will change and who may be joining the decision committee that they need to learn more about.

Rather than the chaos that might have ensued at the acceleration of the timeline, each member of the team is applying critical thinking and trying to help their cross-functional colleagues. The continuum approach to digital marketing is built to have the flexibility that enables scale as needed. By starting with personas, the team will be able to identify changes to existing personas based on the new capabilities the integrated product will bring. Recognizing that a new stakeholder exists and working to identify that persona first will serve to create new understanding and perceptions about the dynamics of the decision process for their buyers.

It's interesting to note, as well, that when Scott informed Diane about the accelerated timeline, he didn't ask about lists or mention lead volume or dictate the type of content needed. He asked for lead generation programs because the leads the marketing team has been generating have been well received by his team, enabling them to win more often. Marketing has earned credibility with the executive team and across the organization for their contributions to revenue-producing activities.

CHAPTER 20

The Dynamic State

In the dynamic state, marketers have helped infuse the entire organization with customer obsession. They have evolved the predictive capabilities acquired in the perceptive state closer to real-time applications that enable them to take the right actions quickly based on insights from data. The marketing team works closely with sales, product management, customer service, and IT teams to ensure that all touchpoints are relevant during the prospect-to-customer-to-advocate lifecycle.

Dynamic marketers realize that the continuum is a virtuous cycle that requires continuous learning to improve the merging of customer goals with company goals. Competitive advantage relies upon dedicated attention paid to this unwavering alignment. No longer are marketing initiatives operationalized as stand-alone initiatives. Activity in each channel is carefully orchestrated and monitored in relation to the others in play. The idea of trying to justify social media activity without considering its relationship to related efforts in other channels is viewed as irrelevant, for example.

Conversations now cross channels in a heartbeat. Our audiences turn to digital devices and channels first, and their expectations escalate along with their newfound capabilities to learn, play, and work aided by technology. Lines have blurred, bringing elements of the personal experience into the professional experience.

To keep pace, marketers have become digital cartographers, social scientists, and data analysts. They have learned to map customer experiences—not just to assign content to lifecycle stages. They have become competent digital conversationalists adept at engaging prospects and customers based on understanding how and when to answer their most pressing questions within a relevant context. Dynamic marketers understand which actions their audiences will be willing to take based on the value and relevance they will assign to each interaction. Marketers have proven that digital relevance is the imperative that helps the company find and capitalize on new opportunities to drive growth and business objectives.

A Day in the Life of a Dynamic Marketer

Diane marvels at the difference in the company's go-to-market approach since she joined Cloud Widgets six years ago as the Director of Demand Generation. Today marks her one-year anniversary as Executive Director of Cloud Widget's Center of Excellence (CoE) for Digital Customer Experience. Charlie, their new CMO, has invited her to present a review of the last year's operations to the executive board.

Diane takes a deep breath before she enters the conference room. The CEO is at the head of the table flanked by Scott, now the Chief Sales Officer, and Harry, the CFO. Also at the table are the Senior Vice President of Customer Experience, the CIO, the SVP of Product Management, and Charlie, her boss. The side conversations among them wind down as Charlie rises and walks toward her.

"You ready?" Charlie asks her quietly.

"As I'll ever be," Diane replied and smiled.

Charlie turned to face the group. "Everyone here knows Diane. She's done a fantastic job with the Center of Excellence and, as today marks one year since we started the initiative, I wanted to invite her to present an update on her team's efforts. Diane, the floor is yours."

"Thanks, Charlie." Diane, buoyed by pride in all her team has accomplished, has decided to forego her slides—at least for now. "I'll start with the high points. Based on the sentiment analysis that Alan just completed last week, positive awareness for Cloud Widgets is at an all-time high. Our year-over-year growth rate in customer acquisition has reached 62 percent due to the work Scott's team has done. And his salespeople have used 82 percent more of the content and collateral we produce than they did a year ago. Feedback has been solid, and they're providing great insights in the weekly standups. A year ago, we were lucky if we could get a couple of salespeople in the meetings. Now, we see at least ten, sometimes more when a product update or launch is coming up."

"I've heard great things about the new process and content portal the center has put up for them." Scott says. "Our customers are reporting that the sales team is bringing more value. In the last two win reviews I've done on accounts, the customers have said that a big reason for their choice was that they felt that their account team really 'gets' them."

Diane can't help the smile that blooms. She really wants to do a fist pump, but resists. "Thank you, Scott. Additionally, the nurturing programs that Mike is running have really gained traction. Our persona work has benefitted from the quarterly refreshes, helping us fine tune our content and messaging. And buy cycles are now shorter by 42 days, indicating that our calls to action and story line are now unfolding in a way our buyers find compelling. We can track patterns of behavior activated across multiple channels, and Susan's team's ability to be hyper-responsive to help connect our audiences to the right content at the right time in social channels is proving to increase engagement that leads to conversions."

Evan, their CEO, says, "What is the most significant industry change you've seen our customers responding to?"

"Speed in application development and delivery is what we're hearing from the sales team, and we're seeing content related to that topic perform better than the content related to cost reduction, which was big at the beginning of the year. Our proprietary process embedded in the platform is a differentiator in comparison with other options."

"That's what we've found in our customer focus groups, as well," Jerry, now SVP of Product Management, agrees.

Diane directs her gaze at Sally, their VP of Customer Experience. "Susan has been doing coaching with the customer service managers to help them teach their agents how to apply our messaging in a 1-to-1 conversation on social media. A report from our contact center vendor shows a 27 percent increase in customer satisfaction after a social service exchange."

"We'd like to think that also ties to our retention rate growing to 92 percent this year," Diane says, glancing around the table, relieved to see heads nodding in agreement. Additionally, the customer service team's insights have helped us create FAQ and self-service content that's seeing much higher engagement than in the past. Call center volume has been reduced by

15 percent. While we can't take all the credit for that," Diane nods to Jerry and Sally, "we'd like to think that helping customers find the answers to their questions in a self-service format is a big contributor."

"I think Harry will be happy that the reduction of outside agency use has been a wash with the operational costs of the center, stabilizing costs. Now that all the systems and processes are in place and have been proven, I believe we'll find additional efficiencies during our next year of operations."

Diane isn't surprised that Harry only looks somewhat appeased. He is constantly on the search for economies of scale. "I have to say that I'm impressed by your ability to manage the budget for the center. But I will need to see improvements next year."

"I'll get them for you, Harry."

Making the Transition

The dynamic state is dependent upon real-time or near real-time responsiveness, and is a natural progression from the perceptive state. By pulling cross-functions under the same umbrella with a CoE, collaboration has enabled the coordination of collective efforts to transform how Cloud Widgets builds relationships with buyers and customers. The charter for a CoE is to set the vision and positioning for the content that will be published and to oversee digital strategy as tied to business objectives. Content and how it's orchestrated across channels plays a critical role in achieving the "humanness" required to truly resonate with online audiences.

In this scenario, the CoE had executive support from the top down and the commitment to apply the time and effort necessary to achieve an impressive transformation. While each function is responsible for setting overall goals and departmental strategies, the content and digital strategies to achieve engagement that moves the needle is orchestrated by the CoE to ensure consistency and relevance in the messaging and digital interactions. One team responsible for sharing the company's story—in line with cross-functional business objectives—results in higher performance than when marketing efforts are distributed across divisions, product categories, or industries the company serves—and subject to differing interpretations.

Reaching a true dynamic state will also require the upgrading of digital marketing skill sets. A combination of customer intelligence, technology competence, predictive data analytics, editorial, and writing chops is needed for excellence in execution. Marketers in the dynamic state have achieved radical relevance, the highest level of the RMM. While many of these skill sets are acquired along with the progress made in each state, it's the shift in how they're applied as each transition occurs that allows marketers to become truly dynamic.

SECTION 6

Contextual Connections—The Art of Getting Personal

Analyst firm Sirius Decisions has been known to say that the reason salespeople don't hit quota is because they fail to articulate value their buyers care about. And marketers who fail to produce qualified leads, accelerate the buying cycle, and improve customer retention suffer from the same ailment. Digital relevance is about context, plain and simple.

Context is most easily explained as the set of circumstances that influence behavior, perceptions, and attitudes in relation to a specific situation. One example is the expectations for a person who types a query into a search engine. Based on the descriptions presented in the search result, the person will either select a link to click on or enter a new query to narrow the gap between what she wants and the choices that the search results returned.

Another example is the way a customer service executive would approach customer experience in comparison to the way an application developer would view it. The service executive is focused on the people, and the developer is focused on the people's interaction with the technology. The depth of understanding that marketers have about what their prospects and customers want or expect from them will determine the relevance and success of their marketing programs.

Companies often approach me about creating content marketing strategies. The first question that I ask is whether or not the company has developed personas. Sometimes I hear that they have, sometimes I hear that they have not, and sometimes I hear that they don't see the need. In nearly all cases, when I ask them to give me a thumbnail sketch of their target audiences, I often hear titles as a conclusion without many supporting details.

I have to ask, *How do you develop strategies to engage, nurture, convert, and retain people you don't know?* It's like trying to plan the conversation you'll have with a blind date. You don't know their interests or preferences. You have no idea what's important to them. You don't even know whether they're a potential match given your picture of the ideal date.

Luckily, on a date you're only dealing with one person at a specific place and time. But a buying situation is different. There are multiple people involved, each with their own perspectives, needs, and goals. Based on their role in the organization, they have different levels of influence and authority. Each of them may come into the buying process at different times or stages. The channels and content formats they prefer may vary, as well as the types of information they need and the questions they want answered.

Personalization amplifies the ability for marketing programs to gain traction. Personas are the active tool that informs the matching of the context of the target audience to the interactions presented in the execution of the digital strategy. Engagement is built as accuracy improves. But it's not just about engaging one of the personas represented in a buying scenario. Context is also needed to enable marketing programs to promote conversations among the people on buying committees to invite them to incorporate your company's ideas and expertise as they deliberate and discuss viable options.

The charter for marketing has expanded based on the digital proficiency of buyers. While a variety of research reports has found that buyers are anywhere from 57 percent to 80 percent of their way through the buying process prior to engaging with a salesperson, marketing is now in a position to help their sales teams better articulate value—and do so earlier in the buying process. The ability to make contextual connections with prospects and customers will elevate marketing's ability to get its company's ideas and expertise absorbed into the marketplace as the definition of value for what it helps its customers achieve. Contextual connections will propel your company's ideas into becoming your prospects' and customers' imperatives.

CHAPTER 21

Engaging Diverse Audiences

"Engagement" is a term that gets bandied around a lot. The term is used in reference to clicks, email opens, page views, time spent on page, new followers, social shares, and a variety of other point-in-time activities.

I'd like to suggest that engagement is not about point in time. It's about longevity and sustained attention based on understanding and responding to what customers care about that results in a mutually valuable relationship. If it weren't, then lead nurturing wouldn't work. And it does. If engagement were about a point in time, then it would follow that one interaction should persuade a prospect to speak with a salesperson. But that's not usually true.

Marketers with whom I work have lengthy sales cycles, ranging from 9–18 months and growing longer. Salespeople say that they're not getting into conversations until much later in the buying process. Buyers say they are viewing more content assets during their research and consideration process. According to the IDG Customer Engagement Study, each buyer views eight content assets, on average, during their buying process.[1]

Therefore, engagement represents more than a point in time. In fact, if the average of content assets viewed is eight, then the engagement challenge would be to increase the share of attention won from your prospects for those eight. If prospects are reading more of your content, then they are reading less of your competitor's. It's also interesting to look at the average number of assets viewed as a multiplier. For example, if your digital marketing programs include a focus on three personas, then gaining a majority share of the 24 assets the group views would bode well in your favor.

The ability to measure engagement is what lead scoring was meant to do once marketers gained the ability to move beyond demographics to activity data. However, it's not that simple in execution, as each type of activity is not indicative of the same intensity of engagement. Measuring activities as if they have the same meaning can lead to misinterpretation of the prospect's intent and state of sales readiness.

For example, if a prospect visits your website and bounces around, viewing five unrelated pages, is he engaged? What about a prospect who arrives, clicks on a topical content asset, and then follows the path created by a thread of links to related content that delivers a story line about how to solve a priority business problem? There is a noticeable difference in intent in the two scenarios, and arguably, in the level of engagement achieved. However a scoring method based on an equal score for the number of pages viewed will reflect both prospects as equally engaged, when logic (and likely reality) would argue this is not true.

Engagement is about what comes next, not simply a moment in time. The concept is also reciprocal. If your audience engages with you, you must engage with them in kind. Otherwise the engagement will stop.

Relevance for One Audience Is Irrelevance for Another

Digital marketers have the responsibility of addressing many different audiences for a variety of reasons. The same messaging and content will not work for all of them. Consider the differences in the following audience types:

- **Prospects** need to know why a problem is worth solving, how solving it will benefit their company, and what impact doing so may have on their career—if the solution works, or if it doesn't.
- **Customers** need to know they're important to you and that you've got their backs as they use your products to achieve the value you promised them at purchase.
- **End users** need your product to help them do their jobs better.
- **Advocates** need for their support of your company and the referrals they make to their peers to reflect well on them.
- **Influencers** need to see the value they'll gain personally from evangelizing for your company in relation to something about which they are passionate.

The interesting thing about audiences is that one person may represent more than one audience type. A customer could also be the end user of your product and an advocate for your company, for example. This adds a layer of complexity to designing engagement strategies.

When you consider that for every audience type there are subtypes, the challenge of relevance intensifies. If you target five buyer personas, then you have five prospect audience subtypes. Understanding that each persona will have a different perspective creates demands for specific content to engage each one. Take the following five personas that comprise this buying committee for a project management solution, for example:

- **Fred, in product development,** is championing the purchase of a project management solution to promote collaboration within global teams in order to shorten time to market.
- **Jane, in human resources,** is worried about training and user adoption issues that could limit the ROI of the solution Fred prefers.
- **Sally, in customer service,** has concerns about how this will impact the ability of her staff to support product launches by creating another silo of product information with limited accessibility for her team due to a lack of integration options.
- **Tom, in IT,** isn't convinced that the security provided by the solution is comprehensive enough to ensure data protection of the company's intellectual property used during product design.
- **Mark, in finance,** thinks the total cost of ownership is too high given the concerns of the other members of the buying committee.

Each of these subtypes—or personas—within the prospect audience type will require a unique approach. While this increases the complexity, the benefit in knowing each subtype is that you can then help Fred have a better, more informed conversation with Tom or with any of the others who must reach consensus to buy.

If you serve customers in different industries or serve both SMB and enterprise companies, you have a number of customer audiences to address. What may be relevant to an SMB audience, may not apply to an enterprise audience. The hierarchy is different, their resource levels are different, and their objectives likely have differing levels of complexity to achieve.

While this may sound overwhelming, what's really important is for marketers to understand and recognize the differences, and focus on being meaningful, given the audience at hand. Doing the foundational work for personas and digital marketing strategy should be based on gathering the insights needed and applying them to execution plans. If your resources are limited, it's far better to be relevant to one audience than to try and tackle all of them, yet achieve relevance with none of them.

Engagement Is about Curiosity and Driven by Context

As marketers plan for each type of audience engagement, they must factor in consistency and longevity. The story they share with each audience must build across lifecycle stages by creating anticipation for what's next. There is always something that is next. In a buying situation, this means guiding them to develop an understanding for how they'll get the outcome they want with your help. In a customer situation, this means showing them how they'll get more value than they originally purchased by continuing to partner with your company.

Curiosity is a driving force in engagement, and it's an emotion related to the thirst for knowledge—or inquisitiveness—that marketers can capitalize on to attract attention at the start of a relationship. When an audience's curiosity is aroused, they are more likely to consider ideas that reshape the way they think about a concept, inviting them to ask new questions related to exploring the nature of a problem or an objective. This exploration sets the context that will shape their curiosity.

While prospects may be interested, if their curiosity isn't piqued in relation to something they need to achieve, that interest will diminish or be transferred to another topic because they're not intent on learning more. Curiosity will prompt prospects and customers to ask questions, raise concerns, or ask for advice. Interactivity is necessary for creating engagement that results in building relationships. As relationships develop, curiosity should transition to intent. When your audience engagement strategy is designed to be responsive, the result for your prospects and customers is empowerment because they are driving the conversation based on their agenda, not yours. This sense of control for buyers is one factor that aids in the progression to intent.

Relationships are a two-way exchange. Marketers must also maintain a curiosity about their audiences. One of the most difficult things to achieve is a flexible mind-set and digital strategy that enables marketers to develop a comfort level and confidence in letting go of the idea of control. Realistically, the only person in control is the buyer or customer. They are the one making the choice. We can guide them, but there's a fine line between guiding and pushing. Marketers must respect the difference.

By being curious about audiences, marketers are able to discern new developments and opportunities beyond the messaging you've created. You'll find nuances in the "story" that can be used to adapt on the fly and become even more responsive without veering from your brand's positioning. Building this level of flexibility into your digital marketing strategy requires some anticipation and preparation.

Build a Conversational Framework

Conversational frameworks based on questions that may be raised by the variety of audiences that marketing programs serve can help improve your readiness to become more responsive.

Conversations naturally follow a question-and-answer format. To create a conversational framework for a specific audience requires that you know the potential questions that could comprise the dialogue a digital marketing program is working to establish. As shown in Figure 21.1, it's important to consider that questions may be answered in more than one way, depending on the contextual differences marketing teams have identified across audience types. The answers in your framework become the premises for content development. The upshot is that conversations are synonymous with engagement. If there is zero engagement, there will be no conversation.

It's easiest to define each audience's questions during the persona development process. This is when marketers are engaged in learning as much as

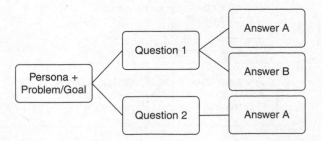

Figure 21.1 Conversational Framework.

they can about each unique segment of their target markets and when they're speaking directly with buyers who have become customers. Salespeople can also provide valuable input when asked about the types of questions prospects and customers ask.

Creating a conversational framework based on questions also makes it easier to determine the flow. You wouldn't start a conversation by saying, "Will you let me know what you find out from Sally when you talk to her next week?" This question would most likely come toward the end of the conversation after you've discussed why the other person is going to speak to Sally and about what. The same sense of order is true for your audiences.

Once you've developed the questions and answers that you anticipate as relevant to your conversational framework, you can play them out with conversational modeling to assess the flow of the informational exchange. Conversational modeling is the equivalent of simulating a conversation based on what you know about the audience.

In the conversational model represented in Figure 21.2, you'll see that following the thread does make sense and establish context. Your audience wouldn't ask the third question about other ways to solve the problem if they hadn't gotten an answer that satisfied the first question about why they should care. Once you've done conversational modeling, you're ready to develop the content that will serve to answer each of the persona's questions. Just be aware that there are many different paths a conversation can

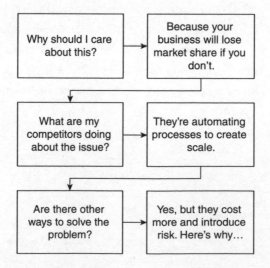

Figure 21.2   Conversational Modeling.

take. Start with one model, test, and refine. Make adjustments and repeat. Iteration is the key to developing effective conversational frameworks. And it's very difficult to create them in a vacuum. You won't know how well they work until you use them with real audiences.

The need for flexibility becomes clear when marketers realize that prospects don't always start at the beginning. This happens when they get answers to earlier questions elsewhere. However, by developing conversational frameworks designed to address the prospect's context in relation to the problem they're solving, it's fairly simple to pick up the conversation in stride. Rules can be programmed into marketing automation systems that trigger the next piece of content based on the last piece with which the prospect engaged or the content that raised their curiosity enough to get them to fill out a form.

By anticipating the conversations that will serve to engage each audience, marketers can become better prepared to respond with a relevant dialogue. Building a conversational framework and model takes time and effort. But once you have it, evolving engagement based on patterns of behavior identified in the activity data for that audience is simplified, allowing marketers to strengthen relationships at key points in each stage of the customer lifecycle. These tools will also inform how marketing teams can participate effectively in a variety of channels given the unique characteristics of their target audiences.

CHAPTER 22

Establishing Digital Relevance
Across Channels

L ife would be simpler for marketers if their companies still owned all the channels in which they were expected to participate. But in this day and age we are all leasing real estate on channels we don't own, such as Facebook, Twitter, LinkedIn, Pinterest, YouTube, Google+, and others. Unfortunately, this has resulted in marketers rushing to use external channels as broadcast outlets in an attempt to pull audiences back to the digital properties they own, including their websites, blogs, microsites, and company-sponsored community portals.

Forcing traditional marketing methods to adapt to digital channels is not the best approach. However, in an attempt to keep pace with competitors and rise above the noise, marketers have responded by developing more and more content and pushing it out everywhere they can, as fast as they can—often without regard for relevance. Rather than the rallying cry for "more," marketers should heed the amplifying demand for "better."

One reason for this flurry of activity is that CMOs aren't measuring cross-channel efforts in a relational way. Only 21.6 percent of marketing executives surveyed said they were doing a good, or very good, job of measuring the impact of one channel on the performance of another.[1] One example could be the impact of display advertising on search marketing.

The ability to measure apples-to-apples impact is also sketchy, with only 10 percent of marketers using the same KPIs across all channels. This makes it difficult to evaluate channel performance in any meaningful way in relation to overall digital marketing strategy. Although marketers are embracing more and more channels in their digital marketing execution, only about 25 percent of them can identify and measure the combination of touches across channels that will result in more conversions.[2]

What may be surprising in this study overall is that only 13.9 percent rated content creation as a very important short-term priority, even less, 8.2 percent, rated multichannel execution as such. CMOs have either determined that they have enough content or they're retrenching to formalize strategy for digital marketing due to an increased need for accountability for performance and business impact that they are thus far ill-equipped to prove.

Personalization is a key factor in establishing relevant dialogues across channels. Unfortunately, this appears easier said than done. Seventy-six percent of marketers interviewed by Forrester Research indicated that they struggle to optimize campaigns based on customer interactions. The same marketers also have difficulty selecting content relative to the customer's context.[3] Interestingly, a similar survey found that CMOs' top worry was their ability to create sustainable and engaging customer relationships.[4] Given the findings above, it appears that CMOs have good reason to worry.

Cross-channel, integrated digital marketing is not for the faint of heart. Failure at relevance in channels arises most often when they are treated as silos, without marketers taking care to connect the dots or address the relevance for the audience's overall experience. Part of this is due to a lack of technology and usable insights from data, but much of this disconnect is due to the lack of cohesive, integrated strategy in support of digital execution, as well as an evolution in the marketing team's skill set.

Channel Characteristics Influence Relevance

Just as audiences come with expectations, the characteristics of the channels in use help set those expectations. Intent plays a big role. Consider why people may choose to interact in certain channels. For example, Facebook is highly personal, whereas LinkedIn is a professional networking site. Twitter is for short snips of information intent on garnering mentions or presented with links to motivate clicks and retweets. Instagram is the place to go for pictures. The corporate website, while a haven for product information, is expected to be helpful, but is also recognized for a bias in favor of the company it represents. The corporate blog is expected to have more personality and be more conversational than the website, but also to let the personalities of its authors to shine through.

While marketers have adopted many channels, they haven't put a lot of emphasis on learning how to use them effectively. That only 42 percent of marketers rate their content marketing efforts as effective serves as evidence of a lack of understanding of how to use integrated digital marketing to establish a competitive advantage. Overall, marketers use 6 social media platforms and an average of 13 tactics. While marketers are struggling to prove effectiveness, only 64 percent of them rank engagement as a top organizational goal.[5]

Digital channels are dynamic. The channel your audiences are most fond of this year could be a virtual ghost town the next. Marketers must focus on finding the right blend of channels to create cross-channel engagement that results in memorable experiences when taken as a whole. The most important thing to remember when planning for a mix of channels is that it's not about what you like, but what your customers want and will appreciate. You may absolutely love Facebook, but if your audience prefers a mix of LinkedIn and videos on YouTube, then Facebook may not play an effective role in your marketing mix.

The reason it's important to look at the mix as a whole is that some channels are difficult to commingle. For example, if your Facebook page is known for great product pictures and fun, interactive surveys, posting more serious articles or white papers there can result in confusion or irritation with the audience you've built for the lighter content.

One example of trying to present an integrated campaign, but misreading an audience's expectations, occurred during Audi's #PaidMyDues promotion. When Audi launched its new A3 sedan, its goal was to broaden the audience for the car. It decided to celebrate resilience with triumphs over adversity and invited people to share their stories via a variety of social channels. Audi enlisted 15 leading artists, filmmakers, and musicians who would take inspiration from the stories to create works of art that would then be auctioned off for charity during a live streaming event. It was a highly successful event that showcased a unique way to incorporate user generated content (UGC) and create emotional connections with the broader audience the auto company was seeking to reach.

Or was it?

eConsultancy included the upset over #PaidMyDues experienced by Audi's fans on Instagram in their recap of the worst social media fiascos in the first half of 2014.[6] The post points out the disconnect that Audi created for the audience on Instagram, who were obviously not thrilled that the pictures of cars they craved were being supplanted by pictures of the artists, filmmakers, and musicians intended to promote the #PaidMyDues event held on May 7, 2014. The audience was confused and posted repeatedly that they wanted cars, not art.

Even though in this case Audi was still posting pictures on Instagram—the purpose of the site—they changed the context without considering that their audience didn't want them to. And, rather than stopping the #PaidMyDues campaign to give their audience what they wanted, they kept posting up to the day of the event without responding to any of the comments to explain their actions or inform the audience what the #PaidMyDues event was all about. While the campaign was integrated across channels and supported by a microsite[7] dedicated to it, expectations weren't set appropriately for the Instagram audience. Audi also showed a lack of responsiveness by never clearing up the confusion expressed by users, or even acknowledging their complaints—some of which were pretty heated. This is an example of why the characteristics of both the audience and the channel must be considered. Instagram is for showcasing pictures, but Audi had set expectations that the pictures on their account would be of cars.

On the professional networking site LinkedIn, the people who use it say they do so to keep up with industry trends, discover new ideas within the industry, establish relationships with colleagues or clients, and build their own reputations. The top type of content that engages them and that they share are research reports, followed by breaking industry news and case studies.[8]

The marketing mix can no longer be executed in a vacuum. Relevance isn't determined by place or channel without considerations for audience. Likewise, some topics are better received in channels that set expectations for them, including the tone, voice, and level of depth presented in the content. This is yet another reason a digital strategy is becoming an imperative.

CHAPTER 23

Goals—Merging Yours with Theirs

The goals of marketers often appear to be at odds with the goals of prospects and customers. In many cases, the goal of marketers is to get a form completion so that they can send the contact to the sales team as a lead. Fifty percent of surveyed marketers reported doing so, and 63 percent indicated the purchase of early-stage leads was included in their lead generation process, which provides 50 percent of the leads that nearly half of marketers produce for their sales teams.[1]

The practice of sending contacts who complete a form to sales as leads has been going on for years. It is one reason for the lack of alignment between marketing and sales, and the basis for the often-heard refrain from sales to marketing that the leads they send them are not worth pursuing. It is difficult to change this mind-set to apply a higher priority to quality over quantity because sales clamors for more leads and marketers are often evaluated based on the quantity of leads generated during a specific period. This disconnect puts marketers between a rock and a hard place—literally. Even if they see the need for change, if the company they work for doesn't change the way they're measured, then how will marketing evolve? How will they find alignment with what buyers want? How will they be able to get and keep their company in the buying dialogue until the prospect is ready to speak with a salesperson?

The goal of marketing should be parallel with the goal of the prospect or customer they are engaging. But it's surprising how far off the mark marketers can be in determining buyer priorities. Research-based membership organization ITSMA conducted two studies. The first study asked buyers,

"What kinds of information/and or support do you expect from a solution provider's sales reps during the purchase process?" The second study asked marketers the same question to help identify how marketers are supporting their sales teams.

The results were disappointing. The last item on the buyer's priority list was "Help build the business case." However, it was ranked as the top priority by marketers for their buyers. According to buyers, their top priority from sales was for them to "provide product or service information." Yet marketers rated this option in ninth place, at the very bottom of their priority list. Marketers couldn't have made their gap in alignment with buyers any wider. And by pushing this false agenda onto their sales teams, they are doing them a disservice.[2] Buyers are providing a clear indication that they need more education about the products and what they enable before they're ready to build a business case.

To understand how the priorities weigh out for your prospects, it's important to return to the beginning of the buying process to understand how each persona defines their individual priorities. What are they trying to achieve? Whatever their key objective is in relation to what your company sells should define the marketing priority. Education, evidence, and expertise information provided to them should be centered around that priority.

For example, if the persona is a VP of Sales Operations and their goal is to get the majority of their sales team to pull their performance closer to the top 20 percent of the sales team, then marketers need to determine what type of information will help them to achieve that goal.

There are a number of steps in the buying process, but aligning marketing goals with buyer goals means putting what they want ahead of what we want, which is for the buyer to become a qualified lead that sales can pursue successfully. Marketers need to back into this goal by defining the steps prospects will take to get there, along with all the micro goals along the way.

The prospect's status quo is the starting line. This is the situation your persona or prospect finds themselves dealing with today. In the case of the VP of Sales Operations, it could be answering the question, Why are only 20 percent of our sales team beating quota? Based on the question, the goal for the marketer is to develop content that answers this question in a way that addresses context and creates the desire to know more.

Context in this early stage could be based on the firmographics of the type of company targeted. An enterprise company with thousands of salespeople will appreciate content that helps them understand what you sell will gain adoption by a wide variety of sales personalities, whereas a small company with a sales team of five may be more interested in how fast they can see results, for example. If you've created content that your persona finds relevant, you'll earn the right to answer the next question on the persona's path to choosing the best way to elevate his sales team's skills. Each interaction should focus on getting permission, buy-in, and anticipation for the next one. The buying process must be progressive, or it's really only static browsing.

Mapping Content Helps Merge Goals

The practice of mapping content to buying journeys will aid in the development of relevance maturity. Unfortunately, mapping is still rudimentary in application because it's approached as a "bucketing" task. Content is assessed and labeled to be early, mid or late stage. This is often done for the marketer's benefit in order to identify which content to use based on when or how a contact enters the database or to identify transition points. The content a visitor views is then used as a trigger. For example, viewing a demo usually prompts a follow-up from sales.

While theoretically this makes sense, the approach ignores context because it's based on what the marketer wants to see happen rather than an understanding of what the prospect wants. Did he land on the demo page from a search result for "demo of X?" Or did he land on the home page, click around a bit, and then display curiosity about the product and decide to view the demo? Did he view the entire demo or only a brief part of it? It takes more than one instance of engagement to discern context.

Mapping content to buying stages must be done with a view toward motivating action based on known context. The content assigned to each stage must accomplish a certain level of progress in order to move the prospect from one stage to the next. If prospects are active and then become dormant, your goals may be out of alignment with theirs.

It's one thing to know you have ten pieces of content that apply to each buying stage. It's another to know that the way you present three pieces of content for one persona will satisfy their need at that stage and motivate them to view the content that carries the story forward and moves them into the next stage. Mapping content goes far beyond assigning content to a bucket, irrespective of other content representing parts of the story. Marketers must determine for which channel it's most appropriate and which content precedes or follows it in the continuum.

By ascertaining what your target audience's goal is, you can match it to the goal of the content. Consider these as small goals or questions that—when joined together—will result in the continuum experience. The reason it's called "mapping" is that it helps your prospects traverse a path to arrive at a destination, also known as buying.

It's the Information, Not the Format

One of the first things I hear from marketers in discussions about content is related to the type of content the marketing team wants to create. They get caught up in the format before they think about the topic or function. The place to start is not considering whether the idea results in a white paper or an eBook or an infographic. But many of the reports published about content stipulate that certain content is only used in specific stages of buying. So this is where marketers tend to focus first.

The problem is in the unknowns. For example, sometimes a prospect will want access to an ROI calculator earlier in the process to determine whether the value will be worth fixing the problem. This doesn't mean they're sales ready. It means they are making a choice about whether to continue with their research or to abandon the idea and move on to their next priority. But a number of reports would have you believe that accessing an ROI calculator means late stage and sales ready. The problem with this assertion is that the context is the determining factor, not the format.

I hope marketers will break this habit of assumptions based on formats. Your audience doesn't go online and think, "I really want to find an infographic." They go online with an inquiry, such as "I wonder what other companies are doing to find and retain the best talent for operating marketing automation systems." Will it matter in what format the answer to this question appears? It might. But if you remove format as the focal point, you're now freed up to create content that merges your goal with theirs and that has a much better chance of being perceived as relevant.

Start with the idea and then answer questions, including

- What topic will you explore and for whom?
- What question are they asking?

- What will they get from how you answer it?
- What do you want to accomplish?
- How will the content work within your story line?

With the answers to these questions, you can define a suite of content to develop around the idea or topic, complete with a distribution plan and how you'll connect the dots across channels within the story you're already telling. Instead of one content asset, start thinking in terms of content hubs based on the small goals your prospects and customers need to reach on the way to the big one. Format is not the most important element; rather, information is.

CHAPTER 24

Audience Overlays

Part of the challenge with marketing a complex product or solution is that more stakeholders are involved in making the decision to buy. According to studies, the average number of people involved in making the decision about a considered business purchase can range from 5 to 21. While there is usually one person who holds the ultimate authority to authorize the decision and spend the budget, there are many other factors that come into play. If even one of the stakeholders says "no," the decision to purchase is in danger of stalling or not being made at all.

The task of helping the buying committee reach consensus used to be relegated to the sales team. However, with the prolonged research and time now spent on the front end of the buying process, if marketers don't help facilitate the consensus for each decision needed to move forward, it's likely that your company won't make the short list for consideration.

This is where audience overlays come into play. Audience overlays are the relationships that the members of the buying committee have with each other in relation to the problem being solved and how the solution chosen will impact each of their roles within the company. In a consumer decision, an audience overlay can be the family, peers, or the community. Each person involved will bring their own perspective to the table. Understanding the dynamics of these relationships is yet another healthy argument for depth in the development of personas.

The sales team is focused on building relationships with the decision-maker, but this isn't always the best opportunity. In many of the persona-building projects I've led, the decision-maker is removed from much of the process and relegates the ideation, research, and evaluation to subordinates. So, while salespeople want access to the decision-maker, marketers must pay attention to which audiences their marketing programs can reach and engage. If they do not reach the decision-maker, then audience overlays become even more important as a way of getting their company's expertise and ideas into the discussion before the short list of potential vendors is created.

By knowing the interests of the stakeholders, marketers have a unique opportunity to stimulate cross-committee conversations. Let's say that marketing is working with three personas but understands that there are several additional influencers on the committee who can sway the decision one way or the other. By developing content that speaks to the concerns of the influencers, while honoring the perspective of the persona, you're helping them understand how to discuss the option of solving the problem in a relevant way and how to respond to any pushback they may get from these influencers.

Understanding the dynamics of the buying committee also enables marketers to create pass-along content that the personas marketers engage with their programs can share with influencers. One of the ways that marketers can speed up the buying process and create a smoother path for salespeople is to remove risk from the equation. Quite often, momentum toward purchase is slowed when perceptions of risk are held by one or more members of the buying committee.

Risk manifests itself as what-if questions:

- What if users won't adopt the new platform or process?
- What if the vendor doesn't deliver as promised?
- What if it takes longer to get to ROI?
- What if the new solution requires more change management than we thought?
- What if the new solution requires a new workflow in an adjacent department?

The more of these what-ifs that marketing can resolve along the way, the greater the chance that your company will make the short list and that your salespeople will be invited into the conversation. Addressing audience overlays well can create competitive advantages because your ideas are being used in the conversations that are held without your company having a physical presence. When prospects utilize your ideas on their own to build their reasoning and discuss options, you've gained an advantage over your competitors.

Advantages Gained with Audience Overlays

Creating overlays takes a concerted effort. This can be daunting for marketers who are already stretching budgets and time to address the specific personas their companies have agreed to pursue. But the advantages make the effort worthwhile. And it's important to realize that persuasive and relevant content designed to enable cross-committee conversations doesn't require an entire campaign. It's more of a see-also effort that extends the programs you're already deploying.

Consider a program to engage a director of IT. Perhaps you've been able to identify a system administrator and a help desk manager who will be affected by the purchase decision. If you've created a content hub for the director of IT persona, you have the perfect place to include a few content pieces, such as articles like "How to Help Your System Administrator Make the Shift to X" and "Why the Help Desk Will Benefit from X," for example. If your IT director is being approached by those two influencers, content assets that speak to their perspectives can become highly desirable for your persona.

Higher engagement results when you expend the effort to help your personas become curators of content for stakeholders. It makes them look good to have the answers to questions they may be asked. They will appear proactive for sharing the information and your marketing will have been able to engage more stakeholders without the hassle of creating yet one more dedicated marketing program. Overlays also lead companies holistically toward an account-based approach. With the ability to help the salesperson understand who else may be involved beyond the sales-ready lead, the salesperson will be more prepared to have the right conversation when they're invited in.

Content for Audience Overlays

In addition to the types of articles mentioned above, there are several other types of content that work well for audience overlays. A spin on case studies is highly relevant. But marketers must think beyond the traditional template that includes company background, challenge, solution as a list of products and services, and a summary of results.

Consider how others played a role in the deployment. This could include unforeseen obstacles that had to be overcome and unexpected benefits or value realized post-implementation. Gleaning this type of insight from new customers and follow-up interviews with those involved will help you provide content that discusses ideas that interest influencers without expending the effort to create a full-blown persona.

Remember that you only need just enough content to help your persona facilitate and guide these conversations in a way that helps prospects keep moving forward. Think of influencer content as a subplot to the persona's story in the continuum. And make sure you provide easy and obvious ways for prospects to share it.

CHAPTER 25

Marketing-to-Sales Relationship Architecture

Performance has always been the overarching goal of commercial companies. Improving performance sometimes works and sometimes does not. Most of the time when it doesn't work, it's because learning doesn't keep pace with change. For marketing and sales to form a new and powerful relationship based on the unifying focus of accounts—based on personas—each group must look beyond established beliefs to accelerated learning that can be used to improve performance.

Nothing about marketing or sales is static. At least it shouldn't be. Even when marketing programs are focused on your existing customers, to assume that they are the same as when they originally purchased from you will inhibit success. Very simply, your customers evolve every day, and so must the relationship between marketing and sales in pursuit of new customer accounts.

One shift in mind-set that can bring marketing and sales closer together from the start is to move from a focus on individual leads to a focus on accounts. A salesperson considers all the players when pursuing an account, and marketing can add value with this approach as well. By using an account-based focus, marketing and sales can take a unified approach, which makes building a marketing-to-sales relationship architecture a simpler proposition.

Building relationship architecture involves designing the processes that connect people and direct behavior in pursuit of a common goal or interest. In this case, revenue and customer acquisition and retention are the goals. When designing a new marketing-to-sales relationship architecture, change and learning must be accepted, accelerated, and willingly embraced. Sales and marketing, working together, will be able to create an architecture with the mutual buy-in that's required for successful application.

The components necessary to create a marketing-to-sales relationship that promotes sustainable performance include

- access—leads that are representative of personas at accounts that will invite sales interactions and that sales agrees are worthy of their pursuit;
- connections–how the leads/personas at a targeted account connect during the buying process;
- contextualization–what leads/personas care about in relation to their objectives;
- conversations–how to add value in relation to what leads/personas care about;
- orchestration–facilitating next steps;
- acceleration–speeding time to close.

It's important to realize that the architecture must be permeable. In other words, each of these components will contribute to performance based on the input that's available from both sides to drive continuous improvement. When marketing is driven by accounts—rather than individual

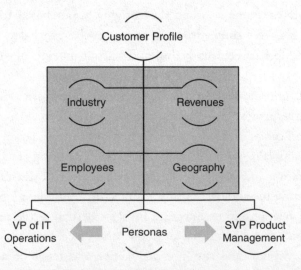

Figure 25.1 The Foundation for Account-Based Marketing.

personas—the focus is expanded to the relationships between the people within an account and how the account as a whole represents a "buyer." Audience overlays, as discussed in the last chapter, were a preview to account-based marketing.

The account also has a relationship architecture that must be understood in order for marketing programs to effectively develop the account to the state of being a sales opportunity. A combination of account definition, buying process, personas, an integrated revenue generation process, technology, analysis, insights, and continuous learning facilitates an understanding of this.

Architecture for Marketing

With account-based marketing, marketers have the responsibility to attract and engage contacts from accounts on a targeted list. The list should be compiled in collaboration with the sales team and based on your company's ideal customer profile as reflected by your best, most profitable customers. Engaging personas related to accounts can be achieved via online marketing programs, including the website, social media, lead nurturing programs, webinars, display advertising, and more. But it also includes offline activities such as trade shows and conferences that have been selected based on expected attendance from the target account list.

By using the ideal customer profile and buyer personas, and by understanding your buyer's journey, you can map in relevant content that's engaging because it helps prospects attain the knowledge and answer the questions that they have at each stage of the buying process.

Technology that can identify the account to which the contact is related and then present content that establishes a contextual connection enables the analysis that informs marketing about buyers' interests. Additionally, their level of activity and stage in the buying process become critical for knowledge transfer that enables better sales access and conversations.

With the ability to monitor the activity of contacts across the account, inferences can be made about the level of overall account interest and urgency. For example, Demandbase learned that shortly before their targeted accounts become customers, there is a noticeable spike of website activity among the contacts from across the account.

Creating the marketing architecture is not an exercise that can be completed during a two-hour lunch meeting with the sales team. It's important to monitor targeted prospect activity and identify repeated patterns and what they mean for acceleration of the buying process over time. But in the interim, it's important to learn more about the sales process and to connect the dots.

You should start discerning which intelligence can be gathered from the marketing process and transferred to salespeople during the handoff that they can use to quickly prepare for pursuit. Similarly, insights from the sales team about the buying process can powerfully inform an integrated marketing plan.

Find out what salespeople need to know in order to quickly articulate the value of your product or solution to gain an invitation for a conversation with an account. This is an extension of the persona development process, with a focus on how to help salespeople step more gracefully into the buyer's process by providing the information, content, and prospect data that they can use to become immediately relevant. Learn about what salespeople need to accomplish and relate it to the buying process that marketers are already guiding. Evaluate your prospects' activities in order to determine which content elements and formats will best enable buyer (and seller) goals.

Based on this learning, determine how marketing can help orchestrate the buying process through relevant content and programs that are aligned with the sales conversation.

Architecture for Sales

Constructive feedback and insights from the sales team as to what they learn in their conversations with contacts at targeted accounts are critical to creating a valuable sales architecture. It also means that there should be a regular channel for communication from sales to marketing about what is working well and what is a struggle in the selling/buying process.

Based on the data available, marketers can perform analysis and make best-case assumptions based on the patterns identified, but the proof is in discovering whether those assumptions match the reality that the contacts at the account are experiencing. Marketers can monitor which combinations of touches and programs lead to revenue, and salespeople can provide another perspective to apply to this analysis and planning.

For the sales team to reap the full benefit from marketing efforts at account-based marketing, they must contribute to the process. Marketers are experts at creating content and collateral that salespeople will find useful if they share the insights from their frontline experiences that inform the development of that process.

Some options for creating the architecture for sales include

- meeting debriefs shared with marketing through an online portal and/ or regular meetings;
- regular surveys about customer and prospect conversations completed by the sales team based on their meetings during the preceding month;
- the creation of a sales liaison who gathers the information through consistent follow-up with salespeople and disseminates the information learned to the marketing team;
- the inclusion of ratings and comments on the sales content portal to allow salespeople to provide feedback in relation to their use of the content marketing provides for sales enablement;
- encouragement of marketers to ride along on sales calls to observe the prospect interaction and return to their team with insights;
- regular meetings to close the feedback loop that include both marketing and sales representatives. You should create an agenda and stick to it. There should be no finger pointing or blame. These meetings must be strictly based on sharing information to improve the marketing-to-sales process.

Salespeople and marketers are partners in revenue generation and cannot function effectively in silos. Many companies have weekly meetings with sales and marketing leadership members at which they consistently evaluate business health through an examination of "one version of the truth" for their end-to-end revenue generation metrics.

All of the above options will provide value, and each one should have a process that has been developed to ensure consistency and timely input in whatever way works best for your team. At the very least, choose one option and start there. Without continuous communication, feedback, and collaboration, the architecture will not be strong enough to endure over time to create a true working partnership.

Use SLAs to Improve Transitions

Finally, Service Level Agreements (SLAs) should be drafted to create a formalized process that sets expectations and requirements for both sides. The key to having SLAs work is that they must provide value for both parties. SLAs can also be useful for establishing KPIs that rate the strength of the relationship architecture by measuring the achievements on both sides in relation to the tenets of the SLA. Attainment against targets for the SLAs can be reviewed in the weekly alignment meetings.

SLAs generally establish the workflow between marketing and sales for accounts based on mutually agreed upon definitions in relation to quality, status, and engagement level. This includes timelines and informational exchanges required at each step of the workflow.

For complex sales, SLAs that govern the development of accounts put responsibility on both sides. This shared responsibility can transform the marketing-to-sales relationship architecture if orchestrated fairly and with the goals of both sides solidly represented. When these goals are created with the nature of the accounts front and center, the selling process will come into alignment with the buying process on the account side. Both of these processes will be empowered through a strategic integrated marketing mix and relevant content for appropriate value exchange, whether through an interaction with marketing or with sales. All of this is needed to create a sustainable marketing-to-sales architecture that moves the needle on revenues.

CHAPTER 26

Social Advocacy

It's just not feasible to ignore the implications of social media for doing business. Companies have had to reckon with the changes in how their customers source information and selectively choose to engage with vendors. Brands now operate under a 24/7/365 spotlight. One of the reasons marketers have been slow to truly embrace social channels is due to the transparency of these channels that's not always kind to the brand. There's an element of risk involved that has required rethinking of how to make meaningful connections with prospects and customers using more channels than ever before. This fundamental shift also includes employees and supply chain partners.

Nearly every channel today, including the company website, involves some form of interaction. Companies and employees alike have established profiles on myriad platforms, and publishing is made possible with the click of a button. Given the implied risk, amplification attached to the brand can be a scary thought if someone doesn't think before publishing. But being left unheard in the channels where your prospects, customers, and partners hang out is almost worse.

Over the last few years, marketers have been charged with "personifying" the brands they represent. This has required establishing a voice, tone, and style for entities that have always stood for what the company ascribed—not based on what the common person thought about it. The need for digital relevance is based on this reversal of roles and impressive shift of power.

The opportunity for marketers is to take up the call to arms by educating and empowering everyone related to the brand to play a starring role in solidifying its reputation. This is not accomplished merely by tweeting the title and link to a blog post or answering a question with a self-serving link to the latest white paper in a LinkedIn discussion group, but rather by identifying conversations to which your brand may contribute authentically amid influencers that may be willing to support it along with the expertise shared. However, attracting influencers requires a bit of finesse.

Attracting Industry Influencers

Experts who have developed industry influence do not exist to advocate for your brand. Each one has their own agenda. What's relevant and motivating for one influencer may not be relevant for another. It is important to understand that you need to establish a relationship prior to trying to engage an influencer in support of your brand. I'm not sure why this isn't obvious, but I can tell you from experience that it is not.

The best way to think about influencers is the same way that a persona helps you think about prospects and customers. What's in it for the influencer? What do they want that supporting your brand will help them gain? There must be a payoff, and I'm not talking about money necessarily. A few things to consider include the following:

- How will the influencer gain from being connected to your brand?
- Will being connected to your brand result in building the audience of people they want to reach?
- Is there prestige involved?
- Will their reputation be improved by advocating for your brand or will they be carrying the load?
- Is there an angle or perspective related to your brand that they can get behind given their body of work in the industry?

Many influencers are consultants who run their own firms. Time is at a premium for them, and what you're asking for in addition to a ride with their personal brand is their time. It may sound like a simple thing to request they sign up for a trial of your product, take it for a spin, and write a "quick" review. However, the reality is that you're asking for at least a few hours of their time. If they sell their time for a living, then you've just asked them to give up income to do your brand a favor. Therefore, marketers must determine whether or not they're establishing that the value the influencer will get is worth their time. This is why establishing a relationship is a prerequisite for a request. It's much more appealing to influencers to hear from a company that has been advocating for them—paying it forward—and that is on their radar than from a company that just shows up in their inbox.

Relevance is critical in establishing this relationship. If you decide to promote an influencer's content as a way of gaining visibility with them, do your research and include commentary that shows them how what they do and care about relates to and supports what your company does and sells. Build the story for the influencer so that when you contact them, it's a pleasant surprise, not an intrusion they have to figure out how to say "no" to. Make it worth their while, and most influencers will reciprocate in kind. The upside about most influencers is that they're truly passionate about what they do. Find that connection, and the odds of your success increase dramatically.

Helping Customers Become Advocates

Customers are the Holy Grail of advocates. However, if they're not happy, they can transform your social clout into a sinkhole. Most companies work hard to create happy customers. Customers, after all, drive business. What marketers haven't adapted to very well is helping customers share their stories or their joy in working with the company and using its products.

Marketers need to create a no-brainer opportunity for their customers to support them. Once again, this is similar to the advice shared above for industry influencers—marketers must consider what's in it for them. However, there is a spin. It's easier to advocate for a person than for a company. Your customers know people at your company. In many, probably most, cases, they do business with your company because of your people. What's needed is to determine how best to help frontline staff engage them on external channels, especially your salespeople. The goal is to make the engagement serve the customer, not the company's agenda.

Social advocacy results from relationships. In some ways it can be a sort of quid pro quo or expression of the Golden Rule: do unto others as you would have them do unto you. The best way to do this is to find out what matters most to your customers. This different from what mattered most when they were prospects. And just as your employees have developed social profiles, it's likely that the people working at customer companies are also working to build their personal brands. How can you help them gain more industry recognition? There's a lot being said about the need for companies to be more human. This is one expression of the concept.

Empowering Employees in Social Channels

One of the biggest opportunities companies have in social channels is to empower advocacy from employees. Marketers should be driving this charge. A few years ago, companies would tell me that their employees weren't using social media because they didn't allow it. Often, it took only moments to find a number of their employees' profiles on social channels. Today, it's pretty much a given that most companies' employees are using social media. The channels may vary, but the point is that employees have a voice. They can use it in support of your company . . . or not mention it at all.

The level of professional participation on social channels—as compared to personal participation—is likely related to the industry of which your company is a part or the amount of support employees have been given by the company. While digital natives—millennials who have grown up with digital—are adept at interacting online, other employees may not be naturals at it. But even if they are, how they represent the brand should not be left as uncharted territory. While marketers are used to brand guidelines and familiar with them, employees are not going to wade through them to learn what's appropriate and what's not. Many of them may have never seen a brand book.

Even more concerning, Gallup's State of the American Consumer Report found that only 46 percent of managers and 37 percent of nonmanagement employees say they know what their company stands for and what makes it different from its competitors.[1] If this is true for your company, there's work to do to achieve brand alignment between customers and employees. There may also be good reason for concern about what they're saying on social media. It's up to you to resolve the confusion. Being on point does matter. The report also identified a 23 percent premium for engaged customers versus a discount of 13 percent for customers disengaged from the brand.

Simplicity in education is the key. Once you're sure that employees across the board know what the company stands for, along with key messages, make sure that it's easy for them to learn the tools and understand how the channels work. Short, ten-minute online courses that talk about one facet of social at a time with a valuable takeaway can help them become better advocates for the company. By employing the option to help employees improve their personal brands, you'll be helping them improve yours, as well.

A few ideas to consider include the following:

- Courses on how to improve a LinkedIn profile, how to participate in discussion groups, how to compose a compelling Tweet, and how to answer a question in a community forum can help set the course for their participation.
- Start an idea bank on the company's collaboration portal or intranet. Seed it with ideas the company should be talking about online and invite contributions from employees. Allow employees to take on the option of developing a blog post on a subject they're passionate about in the idea bank.
- Consider providing templates for different types of blog posts that employees can write and contribute. Demystify the process. For example, a list post is as simple as
  - write an introductory paragraph that explains why your list is important and to whom,
  - list your items, perhaps with an identifier and short explanation,
  - write a concluding paragraph to wrap it up,
  - select a graphic from our account at …
- For every content asset created, provide a brief overview and 10–20 Tweets that can be used to promote it. Or modify this idea for posting to Facebook, Google+, or LinkedIn.
- If your brand is visual, provide graphics on the portal that employees can pin on Pinterest or share on Instagram or embed in blog posts.
- Provide a way for employees to record themselves talking about a specific subject and then have it transcribed, cleaned up, and turned into a blog post with their byline. As they see what's possible from their ideas, they'll be motivated to create more content. Not everyone is a natural writer, but a lot of people can speak very well on a subject about which they care deeply.

Social advocacy should become a core contributor to digital relevance for all companies. But it needs to be facilitated in a thoughtful and meaningful way. Consider options for how best to enable your employees to contribute to the ongoing stream of conversations about what your audiences care about. The difference in brand reach can be dramatic.

SECTION 7

Proving Performance—Science, Not Fluff

One of marketers' biggest challenges is measuring the effectiveness of their marketing programs across channels in a manner that addresses their impact to the business. Marketing programs must "move the needle" to be successful. In order to ensure this happens, marketers must use KPIs that align with tangible achievements, not "fluff" or vanity metrics that are unrelated to business outcomes.

Research by the Fournaise Marketing Group found that 90 percent of marketers have had no formal training in marketing performance or marketing ROI and that 80 percent struggle to prove business effectiveness to their executive teams. That 67 percent of marketers don't believe that marketing ROI requires a financial outcome and that 64 percent use brand awareness as their top KPI are examples of why marketing is often seen as a cost center, rather than a business asset.[1]

Accountability is the toughest mandate for marketers to embrace, as most companies have not required much from them in the past that tied directly to business outcomes. The advent of digital marketing and technology platforms augmented with web analytics and reporting capabilities have put accountability within reach. It's time for the mind-set and strategic application required to prove business value to catch up.

Part of the challenge is that marketers are used to looking at programs based on overall campaign metrics, rather than prospect performance. They've been charged with delivering quantity of leads, not quality of leads. Traditional campaigns were measured in volume of activity, with vanity metrics such as clicks and opens. Each campaign was measured as a stand-alone initiative with start and stop dates that boxed in the results irrespective of other marketing programs in play. The impact of one campaign on another wasn't considered. A webinar running in the same time frame as a conference and an email marketing program covering the same topic would each be measured independently of the impact they may have achieved if the influence of each was mapped to the others. Personas and segmentation were not the norms they're starting to become. Relevance was an afterthought as pushing products and self-serving themes were the driving factors.

This approach is obsolete. The companies that have yet to realize this will be confronted with the truth very soon, if they're not struggling with it now.

The increasing responsibility put on marketers for creating digital experiences that build coveted relationships with prospects is taking center stage. The existing relationship established prior to handoff is costly for salespeople to overlook and can stall forward momentum in a heartbeat, if not handled well. Many companies are taking note and working to create a more informed transition from marketing to salespeople to enable them to step into the conversation with grace and added value.

The challenge that comes from the progress made with digital marketing is in how to measure the cumulative impact marketing programs make on business objectives across all the channels in use. Seventy-four percent of marketers asked agree that converged media campaigns are necessary to maximize marketing effectiveness. But only 9 percent of them confidently stated that their most recent campaign is an example of synergy across paid, earned, and owned media.[2] The report concluded that beyond the rate of change, a contributing factor is the silos in infrastructure and marketing hierarchy that keep marketers from developing an integrated approach. When the demand generation team doesn't talk to the social media team that doesn't talk to the corporate marketing team or the public relations team, you've got not only an effectiveness problem but also a measurement nightmare. That only 28 percent of marketers claim their audiences have a consistent experience with the brand across all touchpoints isn't surprising, but it must be rectified to make progress with relevance maturity.

The fragmented state of the marketing organization raises a few questions about performance:

- How do marketers prove value?
- What value are they aiming to deliver?

- How does what each marketing team accomplishes contribute to overall business value?
- Even more importantly, how can marketers present the outcomes in the language of business to gain respect and strategic leverage with the executive team?

From using data and analytics to harvesting insights to ensuring that the needle is moving in the right direction requires that marketers drill down to the account level. Rather than reporting that they handed off 100 or 1,000 "leads" to the sales team this month, marketers need to be able to say why the leads were passed over, how they enabled the transition, and what factors contributed to the status of a qualified lead. It should go without saying that a form completion is not a lead unless the form is a direct request to have a salesperson contact them.

Marketers need to be able to identify patterns of engagement that define intent across buying stages and demonstrate that by applying those insights they are able to continuously improve outcomes. Rather than benchmarking against the industry, they must benchmark against their historical efforts. But they can't stop there. Marketers also need to show how they enable and support salespeople in gaining entry into more conversations and relationships that result in faster and more profitable customer acquisition and retention. While marketing contribution is often related to downstream revenues, with a continuum approach marketers will be able to quantitatively demonstrate impact at each stage of the customer lifecycle.

This section will challenge marketers to think differently about what they measure and how they manage the continuum approach to digital marketing to gain respect and acknowledgment from the executive team.

CHAPTER 27

Data and Analytics for Business Results

D ata used to be difficult to find. Now there's so much data that it's difficult to manage. When asked whether or not they agree with the statement, "I am able to handle the volume of marketing data that's available without feeling overwhelmed," only 6 percent of 301 marketers strongly agreed. The reasons marketers cited for not using data more include a lack of time to collect and analyze it, an inability to see it in real time, and an inability to see it in one place on the device of their choosing. While 87 percent of marketers say they rely on data to do their jobs well, less than half of them say they have the access to data they need in order to do so.

More than 82 percent of marketers say their bosses expect them to report data-driven results—including ROI—from marketing initiatives, which only adds to the pressure to use data. That only 33 percent of marketers receive reports that indicate contribution to revenues makes this pressure more painful due to a lack of insight into the data required to report on program performance.[1]

Part of the issue with data and analytics is that marketers are stuck in the old ways of measuring based solely on segregated activity from prospects and customers. They are also using measurement simply to report on past performance in isolation, rather than applying insights to predict the potential for future efforts. But marketers also are not usually data analysts. The trick with data analytics is that you have to know what to ask of the data in order to generate insights that impact marketing performance, as well as help improve it.

Because there's so much data now, it's easy to get sucked into the tactical analysis and forego the strategic application, but this can lead marketers down a rabbit hole by taking their attention away from acting on the insights—commonly referred to as "analysis paralysis." Part of this hesitation is caused by uncovering the "what," but not knowing the "why" or how to go about choosing the right action. The way to get started is by selecting smaller bites of data and using them to create pilots or small initiatives with the objective of tying performance to business objectives.

Identifying Business Metrics

Speaking the language of business is an area in which marketers must gain proficiency. As someone who spent fifteen years as a general manager in the hospitality industry and seven years running a technology start-up, I can tell you that it makes a difference if you understand how to build and interpret a profit and loss (P&L) statement. Looking at your programs first from a business perspective will help you identify how to tie them to metrics that the C-suite cares about, as well as the data you'll need to collect to do so.

At the simplest level, businesses need to generate revenues higher than the costs spent to produce them. This means that to transition the marketing organization from a cost center to a business asset, pulling levers that contribute to revenues while also allowing for efficiency improvements is the obvious approach.

Business metrics that will serve marketers well include the following:

Revenues Influenced: This is a big category, and there are a lot of different ways to slice and dice it from a marketing perspective. The most obvious business metrics are net-new revenues and cross- and upsell revenues from existing customers. The sharing of expertise and relevant ideas that help your prospects and customers think differently about how to solve their problems also influences deal size.

In a considered sale, there won't likely be a direct line from a marketing program to a purchase. While the common measures are first- or last-touch attribution, those metrics do little to prove influence over the course of a longer-term buying process. What's required is to prove continuous engagement with content and digital marketing programs that helped the company identify, nurture, transition the lead to sales, and continue to motivate the lead to make progress once a salesperson is involved. By identifying patterns of engagement with marketing assets during the course of buying, as well as the content provided by marketing and used by a salesperson during the process, marketing can validate influence. The ability to prove that marketing is contributing to moving the needle on profitable engagement is benchmarking progress made against historical efforts.

Time-to-Revenue: Over the course of implementing digital marketing programs for a variety of clients, the ability to shorten the buy cycle has accelerated as the programs reach maturity. For example, for one project with an enterprise technology company, a minimum two-year cycle was anticipated for a new market entry with a very complex and high-priced solution. The nurturing program developed based on personas contributed to the company's closing a seven-figure deal in 14 months and four additional similar deals around the 20-month marker. Expediting go-to-market strategies with progressive, personalized content speeds up time-to-revenue and reduces the cost of customer acquisition. Both are outcomes that your CFO and sales team will appreciate.

Retention: Retaining customers is known to be less expensive than acquiring new ones by a large margin. The reasons for this are logical since you've already established a footprint, familiarity, and the delivery of value with the customer. From a measurement approach, customer lifetime value (LTV) is a metric that is important to the business. Digital marketing programs focused on helping customers gain more value than they originally thought they purchased will serve to increase renewals and create additional sales. While attrition to some extent is expected, the lower this number is, the less net-new customer acquisition must be made to achieve growth. Retention programs can also improve social advocacy and referrals. Social advocacy and referrals are becoming increasingly important as more buyers have access to and depend on their peers for credible information on which they can act.

Cost per Lead: For this metric to have meaning, it's important to apply it to only leads that salespeople are willing to accept and pursue. While this will increase the cost per lead as marketers scale the maturity matrix, it's a more realistic expression of true cost. A contact in the database isn't worth very much until that person is in active conversations with salespeople. Approached from this perspective, the metric also helps improve marketing and sales alignment based on defining the qualities necessary for a sales accepted lead (SAL). Rather than measuring on quantity, this metric should emphasize value. And if the leads are higher quality, more of them will convert faster with the potential for larger deal sizes, increasing the revenues influenced by marketing programs.

ROI or ROMI: ROI and ROMI are often considered a purely financial equation—the amount of financial gain less the cost of the program or the annual marketing budget spent. This is a requisite for marketing accountability, but there are a number of factors to consider. As this metric covers the most ground, it deserves a more in-depth exploration.

One of the reasons that determining ROI, or even the more specific ROMI, is that marketing, on its own, doesn't produce an end result that has irrevocable ties to financial gain unless the sale is a transactional one. In a considered purchase, direct and/or inside sales teams are needed to close the deals, and they earn a commission based on recognized revenue. Without true alignment with the sales team and a measurable sales engagement program, it is challenging to connect the dots between digital marketing programs and revenue.

Goals such as increasing web traffic, clicks and opens on email, and lead generation have been mainstays for marketing measurement because these are goals that marketing can track and own with data to back them up. Social media account fans and followers have also taken up residence in this category. This is because these metrics are easily measured, or quantifiable.

Qualitative measurements are more difficult. With content marketing, for example, marketers would like to be able to say that the content they produce contributes to downstream revenues in a considered sale. But how do they prove this? It would take some time and benchmarking to create a baseline to measure improvements against, but it would be well worth the effort. Consider these two examples:

- Leads were not being nurtured by marketing and sales was closing 10 deals per month based on "cold" leads handed off by marketing
- Marketing started a nurturing program for prospects, the leads participated, and the next month sales closed 15 deals. It could be assumed the content used in the nurturing program influenced that increase.

In this scenario, the assumption is also being made that the prospects didn't engage with any other content produced by this company in any other channels and that salespeople didn't do anything differently.

As the channels and tactics in use continue to expand, marketers employing a continuum approach will be best served by developing a way to identify patterns of content use across the buying process by prospects who become customers and amplifying those insights for continuous improvement, as well as using the patterns to validate contribution.

Return on Investment in Content

Marketers spent 33 percent of their overall budgets on content in 2013, with 54 percent saying they planned to increase this spend in 2014.[2] Expenditures this large should be measured against business objectives. However, marketers often claim that it is difficult to identify which content influenced the final decision to buy your product or solution. I'd like to suggest that there's a way to do so beyond considering first or last attribution, which tends to skew true insights. With marketing automation platforms (MAPs), marketers now have the visibility to determine which content a prospect views during their buying process. Even if the lead is anonymous, many MAPs will track anonymous visitor activity and append the profile information to it once the prospect becomes known (i.e., fills out a form).

Rather than looking at the last piece of content viewed before the prospect agrees to a sales conversation or makes a purchase, the marketer can glean more insight by monitoring the "story" that motivated intent and action.

Ask the following questions from prospect activity data:

- How long were the prospects who became customers during a quarter "known" in the database?
- How many content assets did each view, on average?
- To which stages of the buying process were those assets assigned?
- Which content produced by marketing was used by salespeople for the prospects who purchased?

Marketers produce a lot of content with a variety of goals. But the ROI for content will earn the attention of the executive team when tied to business objectives, such as customer acquisition and retention, and new market penetration. Visibility that enables marketing to provide data-driven insights can help marketers focus on demonstrating how digital marketing played a role in conversion with data-based insights, such as the following:

- *For each new customer acquisition, three of the four personas to whom we marketed, engaged with content we provided.*
- *Eight content assets were viewed across the buying process that we can identify, with two assets provided by the salesperson, on average per lead.*
- *The volume of content viewed escalated right before the salesperson entered the conversation for 75 percent of the customers acquired. All but one of them engaged sales during the options buying stage.*
- *The main channels for prospect engagement during the period were the company website, blog, email nurturing, and YouTube.*
- *The common attributes for the companies that became customers include...*
- *The time from a prospect's becoming known and conversion to customer averaged five months for the customers closed in March. In February, time-to-revenue for known prospects was six months.*
- *Based on the content engaged with across the buying process by those who became customers, the story that activated the most intent to purchase goes like this...*

With these types of insights, the value of content becomes a bit less nebulous because patterns can be derived that are common across the new customers. These insights can help marketers validate lead definitions, topics that resonate and influence intent, activity that can trigger proactive involvement of the sales team and information that can be effective to shorten time-to-revenue. Once benchmarked, marketers can work to show improvements in successive periods. Given the state of change, it's critical that marketers use data-driven insights to become more definitive about how they drive continuous improvement that results in higher relevance.

CHAPTER 28

Relevance KPIs

While it's one thing to measure metrics that apply to business outcomes, digital marketers will also find it extremely helpful to create a set of KPIs that help them improve relevance maturity across the digital marketing continuum. That higher relevance maturity translates into improvements to business metrics only makes this approach more appealing. Relevance KPIs serve as a sort of rudder for guiding digital marketing strategy and help marketers build relationships with prospects and customers. Without KPIs to assist in this process, marketers may be tempted to keep relying on instinct, rather than customer-driven insights, thus slowing their progress.

There are three areas of focus: attention, interaction, and intention. The three areas are progressive and iterative when you first begin. Over time, you'll see them overlap, increasing the intensity of the metrics. Together, the three KPIs will help you measure improvements to your relevance maturity.

Attention

Attention is about generating interest that leads to engagement. Attention is a step beyond awareness, as awareness doesn't necessarily require consciousness. For example, I'm aware of NASCAR, but that doesn't necessarily make me a fan or generate any interest in learning more about the races or the drivers. Similarly, I'm aware of Corona beer, but I don't think about the brand at all unless I'm thirsty for a beer. Attention transcends awareness and plays a key role in the continuum. Attention requires that you captivate enough interest to gain a response from your intended audience. For until they pay you with their attention, it's the equivalent of "talking to the hand."

News travels fast, as they say. But in today's context this means that the life span of content can be short lived. There are many posts published online about the diminishing life span of content given the rise in publishing or "noise" online. But relevance has a way of trumping life-span issues. Evergreen content has the potential to attract audiences for years to come.

Catching and keeping your prospects' attention is influenced by several factors:

- **Relevance** is often governed by our unconscious mind. For example, buyer personas are a topic highly relevant to me, but I don't often go online specifically to look up the term. However, when I see something in my content stream focused on personas, I'll pause to see if I have interest in taking a look. Because it's a topic that I care about, my attention is drawn to it. This is why titles and descriptions for content are so important. The words within them will either trigger a relevance response or result in a missed opportunity.
- **Effort** is an instinctive perception. For example, when I click on a link to something that I perceived as possibly relevant, the first thing I think about is what I have to do to get it or engage with it. If I am confronted with a landing page with a form, that triggers immediate thoughts about the effort required, based on the number of fields.
  If the copy on the landing page doesn't reinforce relevance at a sufficient level, prospects will move on. If the content is presented on a web page with long paragraphs and little white space or lots of small type, the perceived effort to read it diminishes the willingness to continue to engage.
- **Credibility** may be based on awareness or past experiences. Credibility goes to trust. What's the trust level that prospects have that your content will deliver what you've promised? And will prospects believe they can trust what the content tells them? A recent survey of buyer's content preferences found that 64 percent of buyers want vendors to use more data and research to support content. Sixty-six percent of buyers said they only sometimes give credence to content produced by a vendor.[1]
- **Presentation** is not one size fits all. The growth in mobile devices and connectivity means that content must render correctly on the device used to access it. If not, your audience will abandon it posthaste.

The other component of attention is engagement. Engagement applies to the level of activity generated within your database, as well as external to it. While engagement is often defined by clicks and views or time spent with the content, the defining requirement for engagement is based on what happens next:

- Is the audience clicking on the call-to-action (CTA) in the content?
- Do they click on embedded hyperlinks within the piece?
- Do they follow your prompts in other channels to come back to view more of your content on a regular basis?
- Do they tend to share your content with their networks?
- Do they proactively visit your web properties to view your content of their own volition?
- Do they spend enough time viewing the content to actually read it? Or are they spending only enough time to skim?

If the sum total of engagement is they come, they skim, and they leave, then engagement is minimal and you haven't garnered enough of their attention to motivate them to do more. Achieving attention is an iterative process. As a metric, consider how long it takes you to achieve attention. What can you do to become more relevant to shorten that time frame?

For example, if it takes five website visits for a prospect to click on a hyperlink or CTA in the content, or to complete a form or share your content with their networks, on average, how can you refine the content they notice to shorten time to response beyond viewing one resource per visit? Take a look to see if the content that catches attention is centered on a specific topic. Can you create more content like that to speed time to attention? The attention KPI is also a measure of how much effort it takes to generate a contact to enter your database. Notice I did not say "lead."

Additional metrics for validation on attention include assessing new contacts to see whether they match the persona you're aiming to attract and assessing the content to score its performance. These metrics will help you correct course sooner, rather than later.

Interaction

Interaction moves the relationship with prospects a step beyond attention. The interaction KPI is based on measuring your ability to establish and sustain a dialogue with your audience across channels. The act of doing so can also help you identify context for the targeted audience or persona.

A simple way to understand the interaction metric is to think of it in relation to content hubs. For an example, let's use a webinar. You develop a topic for a webinar. In addition to email invitations sent to the target segment in your database who will find it most relevant, you promote registration on social channels. Several blog posts are published about the topic that also serve to drive registration. You hold the webinar session and post a question-and-answer follow up to the blog. Next, you repurpose the slide deck to publish on SlideShare and transcribe the webinar to spin it into a white paper with some additional research. You also create a web page to serve as a hub to host all of this content developed around the topic in one place. You've also connected the dots by linking each content asset to another to build a path for consumption, in case a prospect comes across one piece promoted in another channel.

- How many pieces of content in the hub are viewed during each visit?
- How many people who registered for the webinar attended the live session?
- How many questions did the webinar generate during the live session?
- How many social shares can be related to the content hub?
- How many social posts were made during the live webinar?
- How many prospects who attended the webinar also downloaded the white paper?
- How many on-demand views of the webinar occurred during the two weeks following the live event?

Based on response to the "content hub," how many interactions were you able to sustain with each person who expressed interest? Given the topic and the interactive level of the dialogue, can you discern context for the target audience? Are the people who attended the webinar or downloaded the white paper the intended audience? Do they match your persona? Did they engage more with specific content in the hub? If so, does that give you an indication of what about the topic resonates most?

The interaction metric is also useful for gauging your ability to sustain dialogue as it transitions across channels—in essence, your ability to connect the dots for your audience. Evaluate the data that shows you which channels the audience arrived from and which channels they used to share the content with their networks. Did the content stay in the same channel or was it considered high enough in relevance that it was shared across a variety of channels?

In addition to incremental engagement, such as with the content hub anchored by an event, the interaction KPI can be used to measure the dialogue that marketing was able to sustain across the buying process and even the customer lifecycle. A number of companies I've worked with take better care of maintaining interaction with prospects than they do monitoring the dialogue they're able to sustain with customers. If it takes 10–15 interactions with a prospect before they become a customer, how many does it take to sustain the customer relationship? What would it take to reduce the number of interactions for prospects to become customers and build the level of dialogue you hold continuously with your customers? Succeeding with both will contribute to improving the business metrics you can report to your executive team—shorter time-to-revenue and lower customer attrition.

Intention

Gaining attention and increasing interactions are progressive accomplishments. But the ability to motivate intention is the pivotal point in establishing progression toward buying. Intention is about identifying changes to behavior based on higher levels of intensity of attention and interaction that could be the precursors to an imminent buying decision. Intention is the pivot from interaction to the active evaluation of options for solving a problem or reaching an objective by your prospects.

Intention is defined by a narrowed focus and an interest transfer from strategic thinking and inquiry to product and risk evaluation. Rather than downloading white papers or viewing articles and blog posts, the prospect is now looking at demos, reading case studies, and downloading solution briefs. If you've created content in response to anticipated "what ifs?" this is the time it's likely to be in high use to answer questions that can stall forward momentum, such as, What if users won't adopt the solution? Or, what if the solution doesn't deliver as promised?

If you've been targeting three personas, but only one has moved beyond attention to become interactive, you should make efforts to help the other two catch up. Additional influencers from the account may also become known, or you may see the most active personas sharing more content with other stakeholders. This is where assessing beyond the prospect to all activity related to the account can be indicative of the state of intent to buy.

Intention is related to contacts becoming qualified leads for sales handoff and accepted by salespeople for active pursuit. It can also be expressed by the prospect's reaching out to request a conversation with a salesperson or participating in an interactive demo. Essentially, intention is about action related to buying, not browsing and learning. If you are listening on social media channels, you may see prospects asking for feedback from their networks about your company or solution by name, rather than by category.

Metrics for the intention KPI are related to answering questions with data that apply to individuals or accounts, rather than the target segment as a whole, such as the following:

- How many product-related pieces of content and case studies have been viewed in a short time frame by the prospect or account?
- Is the prospect or are the people related to the account accessing financial information, such as ROI calculators, total cost of ownership (TCO) information, or comparative analyst reports on the type of solution you sell?
- Has the inside sales or qualification team had a progressive conversation with the prospect?
- Have additional people from the account been identified as actively consuming content?
- Has the lead's score reached or come close to the qualified threshold based on a spike of activity related to the above questions?

Given the growing amount of self-education and research that prospects perform, the above are all indicative of their reaching the end of what can be accomplished without engaging with sales to glean insights that apply to their specific situation. If prospects present what looks like intention, but refuse to engage with a salesperson, either their priorities have changed or you may have misread the intensity of their behavior. Remember that not everyone will take a linear approach.

Using the intention metric to report that you've identified a number of leads who displayed these behaviors and have been able to activate X number of sales conversations is indicative of contribution to revenue if those prospects convert into customers. The intention KPI will help you develop and refine a repeatable process for moving prospects through the middle of the pipeline that often becomes a bottleneck in the prospect-to-customer process.

Using Relevance KPIs with Customers

Relevance KPIs apply to all stages of the continuum. Once the transition is made to customer, the application of attention, interaction, and intention metrics will need to shift to address the customer's new status quo. The purpose of the metrics will be the same, but the programs they're applied to—whether adoption, expansion, cross- or up-sell—will require altering the questions asked of the data. You will also reap benefits from working with the account managers and customer service teams to develop and refine the application of the metrics to objectives for the customer base.

A few changes to note for each relevance KPI, include the following:

- Attention—Make sure to account for the change in audience. End users, project managers and others who were not involved prior to purchase will require new storylines based on their objectives.
- Interaction—Measure the affinity of your customers in relation to advocacy and referral programs and satisfaction will come into play. Additionally, the metric may also be directed toward measuring the dialogue that marketing can help generate between account managers and customers, rather than between marketing and customers, depending upon your company's customer management processes. Attending your annual user conference and related activities around content for the event also play here.
- Intention—This metric may be most useful around addressing factors that promote renewals and retention, as well as reducing customer churn.

CHAPTER 29

Moving the Needle—Lead Scoring and Progression

Very few of the visitors to your website will be ready to buy upon their first download or interaction with your company. From a digital marketing perspective, collecting a form completion for "gated" content or a registration to attend a webinar or event is often considered the equivalent of gaining a lead. But it isn't. The form completion creates a contact that may have the potential to become a lead. While marketing automation systems provide lead management tools, including lead scoring mechanisms, few marketers are using them to count more than page views and email clicks and to score demographic and firmographic data collected by forms. Marketing automation platforms put vast potential in the hands of marketers. The challenge becomes how to use it to best advantage.

Lead scoring can be made as complex as you'd like, but simplicity in its application can also provide opportunities that help marketers become more relevant. Lead scoring is not about identifying fans of your content, but about qualifying intent to purchase. By combining explicit information—demographics and firmographics—and implicit information—online behavior—marketers have data that can be used to increase their digital relevance across the continuum.

Matching Demographics to Personas

Based on your company's strategy, your personas have been created to enhance the relevance of your approach. As personas are representative of a role, the design of the forms prospects will complete should reflect what's needed to make an appropriate assignment of the lead to the persona options in your database. The shorter the form, the greater the number of prospects who will will complete it. Consider the information you really need to begin building a relationship with prospects—or disqualify them—before creating your forms. Fewer than five fields is optimal for a form that adds a contact to your database.

Obviously you'll need the basics, such as first and last name and email address. For the two remaining fields, give some thought to what you really need to know to begin engaging the person or to evaluate the fit. For example, if your company only sells to small companies or enterprises, knowing the size of the company is important. If your company specializes in specific verticals, the industry is important. If you have a targeted list of key accounts your company is pursuing, the name of the company is important. I'd argue that top priority should go to title or role for persona assignment. If you use a data appending service, then company name would take the second slot because you'll get the size and industry information with the data append. If your ideal customer also uses specific technology solutions, then that might take the final field.

It's Time to Update Progressive Profiling Techniques

Once you have the contact in the database, progressive profiling on additional downloads can help continue the qualification process. Lead scoring has often been approached with outdated techniques, such as using progressive profiling to determine whether the prospect has budget, authority, need, and timeline (BANT). In many of the projects I work on, the people who have been delegated to do the research and evaluation of solutions to a problem may have need and timeline, but often not have budget and authority—two of the criteria most valued by salespeople.

BANT is outdated and also of little use in helping marketers increase relevance that builds attention, interactions, and intention. Instead of asking self-serving questions related to BANT, "which solution are you interested in?" or "would you like a salesperson to contact you?" focus on identifying their interests, priorities, and approach. For example, asking them "what most interests you" with a list to choose from that mixes pains with objectives can also tell you whether the person is motivated by the carrot or the stick.

Examples might include

- increasing the effectiveness of marketing program execution,
- reducing lead leakage from the funnel.

The person trying to reduce lead leakage is motivated more by avoiding loss than by gaining advantage with the pursuit of greater effectiveness. With this knowledge, you will have a good idea of the tone and style of the content that will most resonate with that person.

Progressive profiling is also a representation of your company's orientation. Asking self-serving questions shows the prospect that your company is focused inside-out. It can also reduce the number of completed forms by communicating that your next action will be to send a salesperson to follow up. Asking questions that relate to what your prospects care about shows you put them first. The answers prospects provide to the questions will also help ensure they are in the appropriate nurturing track and served the most relevant content. Before implementing your progressive profiling questions, it's important to consider how you'll use the information. Collecting data that can't be applied to building better relationships with prospects or helping enhance forthcoming conversations with salespeople incurs wasted effort from prospects.

Patience should also be exercised. Many marketers want to learn as much as they can as fast as they can. One obvious misstep is to fatigue your prospects by sending too many messages too soon. The worst offense, however, is sending salespeople after them when such pursuit is unwarranted. This lack of patience translates into self-focus, is painfully obvious, and can be off-putting to leads. If the buying cycle is six, nine, or twelve months long, you'll have plenty of time to learn more about them. Ensuring you'll be relevant enough to earn the opportunity to do so is why you're asking the questions in the first place.

Scoring Behaviors

Implicit scoring reflects the attention, interaction, and intent levels achieved in building prospect and customer relationships. For companies to use lead scoring to advantage, it must first be about relevance and then about sales. While many examples of lead scoring often focus on giving higher scores to product pages and sales-oriented pages, such as demos, with everything else

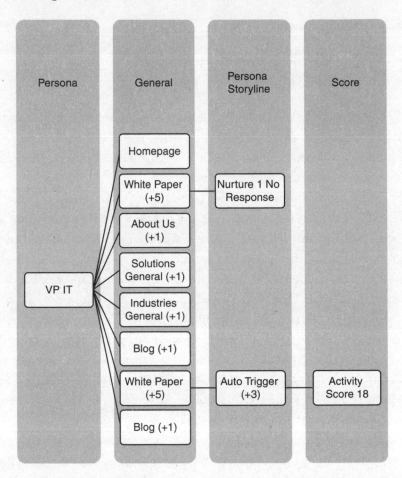

Figure 29.1 Active Persona with No Intent.

scored lower—all web pages visited earn one point, for example—this leaves a lot of opportunity on the table.

The lead representing the VP of IT persona in Figure 29.1 has had nine interactions with your company's content. However, none of them were tagged as specific to his persona story line, with the exception of the content associated with the auto trigger after the second white paper download. Because the scoring is less for random web pages accessed, the total activity score is 18, still too low a level to indicate any follow-up or qualification from inside sales is warranted.

To meet the needs of both marketing and sales, I recommend that scoring be based on a persona with content that comprises a relevant story line, scored across buying stages. To make this work, the content must be tagged

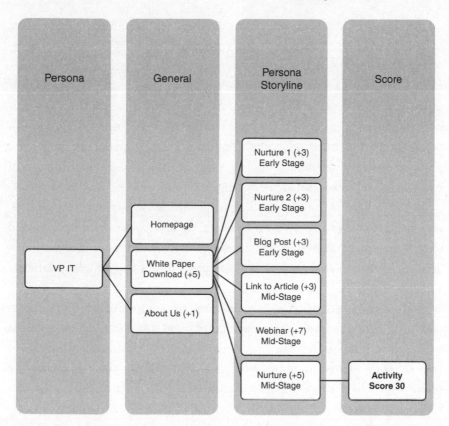

Figure 29.2 Progressive Persona Activity.

by both persona and buying stage, and increment in score as the prospect's behavior shows evidence of progress. At stage transitions, perhaps use an automated trigger to provide an additional piece of content related to content recently viewed and designed to produce additional interactive behavior, such as a white paper with links to additional, related resources. The product content that indicates intent will feed into the stream across the personas, helping marketers identify an escalation of activity within an account and across personas in play.

Figure 29.2 shows the difference when a story line-based score is used with incremental increases as the prospect transitions across buying stages. Note that this prospect has the same nine interactions with your website, but notice the score in relation to the engagement level with the persona story line about solving a problem the prospect cares about. Based on the steady focus of the prospect, his total activity reflects a score of 30, which could trigger a qualifying call from inside sales. The difference in meaningful engagement is obvious when you compare the two scenarios.

By scoring in this manner, marketers will be creating the insight to identify the patterns of behavior indicative of a propensity to buy across the different personas that marketing programs are focused on motivating. This will also make it easier to see whether a prospect has been assigned to an incorrect persona or whether the persona is focused on solving a specific problem or engaging randomly because they're interested in the information you share, but not necessarily in buying.

The data collected on behavioral scoring will also show you where the gaps may be in the story you're sharing or whether some pieces of it have missed the mark entirely. This insight enables marketers to do more of what works and less of what doesn't, as well as to augment stories that could work better by filling a gap that motivates transition to the next "chapter" of the story.

Additionally, this insight will enable you to continue engaging the prospect after they become a customer because you'll understand more about where their interests lie and the types of content that motivate them to interact with higher attention. Lead scoring can help you determine the "cause-and-effect" process that works the best at shortening buy cycles and indicating a prospect more worthy of qualifying calls from inside sales that lead to follow-up from the field.

Level the Playing Field with Scoring

After boosting relevance, lead scoring is about helping marketers identify opportunities to accelerate progression toward purchase. Sometimes contacts acquired are simply that—contacts. They have no intention of buying and should be removed from prospect-oriented persona-nurturing stories. The reason for this is that they skew your metrics without good cause.

For example, you have 500 prospects assigned to the Sally Persona segment in your database. Reporting shows you that 100 of those prospects have become qualified and handed over to sales for pursuit—a 20 percent conversion. What you don't know is that 100 of the 500 are simply content consumers that look like Sally. If they were identified and moved to a general track, your conversion result would become 25 percent for the period and a truer reflection of marketing program performance based on those who participated in each program.

Placing content consumers in the general track allows you to monitor them for behaviors that indicate a change in status may be warranted. But it also allows you to focus on the prospects with the highest propensity to become your customers.

Other than identifying contacts that should be moved out of a prospect program, using negative scores can help ensure that the prospects you think are qualified, really are. For example, a contact who visits the careers page repeatedly or a contact who only visits the website to download the latest white paper or report, but evidences no other activity, or a contact who has gone dormant for several months can be evaluated for score reduction to keep them from reaching the threshold due to the time they've been in your database, rather than the interest and intent they've demonstrated.

A prospect who became a qualified lead, was pursued by sales, and then returned as not ready to buy should also have their score reset to a lower level to ensure that only warranted activity will allow them to requalify in the future. If the salesperson indicates a specific follow-up time frame of six months, then the prospect's score should be decremented by the average number of activities for prospects in the track. Some companies move prospects back to the beginning of the nurture program when they are returned from sales. However, if the prospect has engaged with the materials, it would be better to return them to where they initially exited the program when the salesperson became involved.

Validate Scoring Processes

Lead scoring can be used in many creative ways to provide valuable insights marketers can use to elevate the efficacy of their digital marketing programs and relevance maturity. The most important thing to remember is that it's easier to think through the scoring process and how it will work based on marketing and business objectives that are combined.

Lead scoring is a methodology, and as such you won't know whether it works until you put it into practice. As you see the conversion points develop across the continuum, it's important to measure activity against outcomes. For example, if taking a demo is indicative of sales readiness, how many prospects who took the demo actually became sales-accepted leads? By planning first, you can be sure to devise measurements to validate your assumptions and refine the process as you go. With lead scoring, it's important to think in iterations that lead to higher effectiveness. This will take time and patience, and you may even need to tweak your scoring system until you get it right, but the payoff will be big once you implement this process in your marketing programs.

CHAPTER 30

Empowering Sales with Content

Salespeople don't understand your company's content marketing strategy, they don't see value in your content they can transfer to the customer, and they say it's not helping them throughout the selling process. These are the key insights that came from research conducted by Richardson for its Content Marketing and Sales Effectiveness Survey.[1]

The most interesting finding from the survey is that more than three-fourths of salespeople say they are reading your content. They simply don't know what to do with it or how it relates to the customers to whom they are selling. This could explain why they spend so much time (some studies say up to 20 percent) searching for content—because they're looking for something that makes sense to them—and 63 percent of salespeople say the content produced by marketing doesn't help them generate qualified leads.

The marketing perspective and the sales team's perspective are generally at either end of the continuum. This needs to merge as the two disciplines begin to work collaboratively to attract, educate, engage, and mentor prospects toward choosing your company's solutions over alternatives. The best way I've determined how to help with this transition is for marketing to involve salespeople in the development of personas and get their feedback on the story lines marketing is building to engage prospects. As buyers' habits for educating themselves about how to solve problems and evaluate solutions have shifted, it's as critical for salespeople to improve their relevance maturity as it is for marketers.

In the eyes of our prospects and customers, this means hearing the same value-added story from salespeople as they do from marketing. In fact, your audience doesn't care who's providing the information. What they care about is that it addresses a topic or problem that they've prioritized. With a continuum approach, the story must flow in a consistent and cohesive fashion from first engagement through buying decision, customer onboarding, and throughout the customer lifecycle.

Once marketing has received buy-in from the sales team on the personas and story line, each content piece created should include a one-sheet that helps salespeople quickly understand its purpose and how they can use it conversationally, as well as which related content may serve as a relevant follow-up offer to extend the conversation and elevate the prospect's intent. I call these one-sheet summaries CliffsNotes for Sales.

CliffsNotes for Sales

CliffsNotes for Sales are summaries of marketing-produced content that include the details salespeople need to follow up with a prospect based on an interaction with a specific content asset or to create a new conversation based on ideas that the prospect will find represented in the content if they visit the website.

Components of a CliffsNote include the following:

- Content Details: This is the basic identifying information for the content that includes format, title, a link to where it can be found, date created, author, and, if appropriate, what it was originally created for—such as an event, a nurture program, or a product launch.
- Target Audience: This information helps the salesperson understand quickly for whom the content was created and the stage in the continuum it was designed to address. If the content is specific to a vertical, that should also be included.
- Key Points: Include several bullets that distill the key points made in the content.
- Issue/Problem: This is one sentence or phrase that describes what the persona may be thinking, the problem they're trying to solve, or the objective they're trying to achieve. This information helps the salesperson understand more about the context of a prospect who has engaged

with this content, or content that can be provided if the prospect mentions the issue in conversation.

- Content Goal: A sentence or two about what the content is trying to help the prospect learn or understand that's relevant to the issue or problem.
- Persona Questions during This Stage: Include a few questions the prospect might have during this stage of the continuum, to help the salesperson understand how to evolve the conversation. While this may not be necessary for experienced field salespeople, these questions have proven very helpful to inside sales teams or newly hired salespeople who are still ramping up their knowledge of target markets.
- Answers Provided: Include brief answers to the questions raised above that are addressed in the content as talking points for salespeople.
- Conversational Prompts: Given the content premise, key points, and questions answered in the content, provide several prompts that will help salespeople initiate conversations perceived as relevant by the prospect. These conversational prompts should also lead the conversation toward the collateral and the follow-on offer to create a transition point as the call wraps up.
- Collateral and Follow-on Offer: These are a title and a link to a related content asset with a sentence about it that the salesperson can use to ask permission to send it to the prospect to extend engagement.

The above may look like a lot of work, but if done at the same time the content is created, while the information is fresh in the writer's mind, it takes only a few minutes. Much of what's needed may be in the content assignment document, simplifying the creation of the CliffsNotes further. Providing salespeople with insights about how to use the content that marketing is investing 30 percent of its budget to create is a worthy goal. Figure 30.1 is an example of what a CliffsNote.

The best way to implement CliffsNotes for salespeople is to work on the concept with them. The template provided is an example (see Figure 30.1). Modify it to suit your content and sales needs. By working with the sales team, you'll also gain insights into what salespeople are looking for in content. Knowing their preferences will help you create a one-sheet they will actually use to help them understand how to transfer value from the content that marketing

Item	Description/Guidance
Content Type & Title	• Article – Call Centers Smooth the Way to Customer Profitability – [Link to Content]
Date Created & Creator	• April 17, 201X – Sally Smith
Industry	Financial Services
Persona	Line of Business
Buying Stage	Status Quo
Content key points	• Focus on the customer, not call center efficiency
	• Use the contact center to ask the right questions
Issue/Problem	Customer Service isn't delivering what I need for my product to launch successfully or improve adoption
Content Goal	To show them that research indicates that over-focus on handling customer contacts calls cheaply and efficiently negatively affects the customer's perception of the business or product, and that the call center can provide insights to what customers think and want.
Persona Questions During This Stage	1. What's wrong with my current customer service approach? 2. Why do I need to change it? 3. What will happen if I don't change it?
Answers Provided via Content	1. You don't have the right approach if the agent is focusing on meeting metrics and not handling the customer inquiry 2. The wrong processes could be hurting your business by not listening to, and reporting, customer insights. 3. You're missing out on the opportunity to improve the way that customers think about your products and company.
Conversational Prompts	Talk about what good customer interactions achieve, not the prospect's current call center methods themselves
	• Have you ever considered how much the customer experience affects product acceptance? • What would you say if I told you that changing a few key things could help improve customer satisfaction scores? (Leads to offer of white paper)
Collateral and Follow-on Offer	• 5 Myths white paper [link to paper] • Our VP, Joe Smith, created this white paper following 5+ years of research and projects. I'd like to send you a link to the document.

Figure 30.1 CliffsNotes for Sales Example.

produces to what prospects and customers care about. Remember to make sure they can find the one-sheets or your work has been for naught. Hosting them in a centralized portal is an option that will allow sales to access them easily, and marketing to manage and maintain them whenever content is updated or revised. Helping salespeople get more use out of content will also contribute to a greater return on the ROI from the investment made in marketing content and digital strategies.

Conclusion: Relevance—The Continuous Imperative

Relevance isn't a given. It's not easy, and it's never done. But it is an imperative for companies that want to pursue sustainable business growth. As buyers and customers become more vocal, participative, and demanding, marketers who develop radical relevance will become leaders with a rightful place on the executive team. Digital marketers have a tremendous opportunity to use tools, such as personas, and to take a continuum approach to get attention, sustain progressive conversations, and influence revenues and advocacy that create sustainable growth for their companies.

Storytelling provides the continuous flow from problem to solution, which, when applied with the personalization made possible through personas as active tools, allows for the execution of digital strategy across the continuum of the customer lifecycle. By identifying your company's unique value, as seen through your customer's eyes, you have the opportunity to create a strategy that is not just effective for a specific period but that also has the flex and freedom to evolve your brand well into the future.

Kicking campaigns to the curb is the first step on the path to creating a digital strategy that's continuous, consistent, and that allows all of your marketing programs to work together in concert. By taking a big-picture approach, marketers will be better equipped to engage the C-suite in conversations that matter based on the impact their programs make on overall business objectives. Focusing on isolated campaigns will never allow you to connect the dots in a way that matters most to your company. The continuum approach will.

While making this transition from irrelevance to radical relevance may sound like a lot to tackle, taking the iterative approach will serve you well.

Taking one step at a time will allow you to develop the skills needed to make your advances stick, as well as allow them to be solid enough to build on as you move to the next quadrant of relevance maturity. Adopting an iterative method to continuous change, such as that demonstrated in the moves that Diane and her team made from being reactive to proactive to perceptive to dynamic provides an example that can help you monitor and measure your progress.

Buyers need your help, but will continue to demand more relevance and less effort to use it. Channels will continue to evolve. Communication preferences will morph and shift. But with the tools and skills you learn along the way to radical relevance, you'll be prepared and become adept at continuous improvement processes that enable you and your team to keep pace easily.

So what does the future hold?

If I had to take a guess, I'd say that marketing will become the business drivers. Radical relevance will make you the go-to resource your executive team needs to make better strategic business decisions because you'll become the nerve center of customer obsession.

And that's something to look forward to with great optimism. I have faith. So should you.

Notes

Section 1   Relevance—The Frame for Engagement

1. "The Content Connection to Vendor Selection," CMO Council, March 2014; http://www.cmocouncil.org/download-center.php?id=278&utm_medium=email& utm_source=general&utm_campaign=content-impact-on-vendor-selection.
2. "Over 70% of Marketers (Still) Got it Wrong in 2013," Fournaise Group, January 23, 2014; https://www.fournaisegroup.com/marketers-got-it-wrong-in-2013/.
3. 2014 B2B Buyer Behavior Survey, DemandGem Report, January 2014; http://www .demandgenreport.com/industry-resources/research/2508-the-2014-b2b-buyer-behavior -survey.html#.Uy4Ao4XeQ 0.

1   Irrelevance

1. "The State of B2B Lead Generation, Buyer Zone," November 2013; http://www.buyer zone.com/pages/leads/resource-center/stateofB2B.html.
2. Ibid.
3. "Digital Distress: What's Keeping Marketers Up at Night?," Adobe, September 2013; http://blogs.adobe.com/conversations/2013/09/digital-distress-what-keeps-marketers -up-at-night.html.

2   Shifting Relevance

1. "2013 Highlights: Inciting a B-to-B Content Revolution," Sirius Decisions Blog, May 2013; http://www.siriusdecisions.com/blog/summit-2013-highlights-inciting-a-b-to-b -content-revolution/.
2. "It's Not Content—It's a Lack of Buyer Insights That's The Problem," Sirius Decisions Blog, January 2014; http://www.siriusdecisions.com/blog/its-not-content-its-a-lack-of -buyer-insights-thats-the-problem/.

3   Social Relevance

1. Marketing Technology Supergraphic (2014), Chiefmartec.com, Scott Brinker, January 2014; http://chiefmartec.com/2014/01/marketing-technology-landscape-supergraphic -2014/.

2. Customer Journey Analytics and Big Data, McKinsey & Company, April 2013; http://www.slideshare.net/McK_CMSOForum/customer-journey-analytics-and-big-data.
3. Customer Engagement Study 2013, IDG Enterprise, September 2013;http://www.idgenterprise.com/report/customer-engagement-2013.

4 Radical Relevance

1. "Digital Distress: What's Keeping Marketers Up at Night?", Adobe, September 2013; http://blogs.adobe.com/conversations/2013/09/digital-distress-what-keeps-marketers-up-at-night.html.
2. Global Survey: B2B is the New B2C, Avanade, November 2013; http://www.avanade.com/en-us/approach/research/Pages/Global-survey-B2B-Is-the-new-B2C.aspx.
3. "The Role of Content in the Consumer Decision Making Process," Nielsen/inPowered MediaLab study, Dec 2013—Jan 2014; http://www.inpwrd.com/nielsen.
4. The Content Connection to Vendor Selection, March 2014; http://www.cmocouncil.org/download-center.php?id=278&utm_medium=email&utm_source=general&utm_campaign=content-impact-on-vendor-selection.

Section 2 Positioning for Competitive Advantage

1. "From Promotion to Emotion: Connecting B2B Customers to Brands," Corporate Executive Board, December 2013; http://www.executiveboard.com/exbd-resources/content/b2b-emotion/pdf/promotion-emotion-whitepaper-full.pdf.

7 The Big-Picture Business Perspective

1. Stepping Up to the Challenge: CMO Insights from the Global C-Suite Study, IBM Institute for Business Value, March 2014; http://www-01.ibm.com/common/ssi/cgi-bin/ssialias?subtype=XB&infotype=PM&appname=GBSE_GB_TI_USEN&htmlfid=GBE03593USEN&attachment=GBE03593USEN.PDF.
2. "It's Official: Forrester Says Campaign Marketing Is Dead, Tom Murphy," CMS Wire, April 2014; http://www.cmswire.com/cms/digital-marketing/its-official-forrester-says-campaign-marketing-is-dead-024784.php.

8 Customer Experience Brings Competitive Advantage

1. Meaningful Brands, Havas Media, accessed on 4/18/14; http://www.havasmedia.com/meaningful-brands.
2. Inside the Millennial Mind, Corporate Executive Board, March 2014; http://www.executiveboard.com/exbd/marketing-communications/iconoculture/millenials/millennial-mind-infographic/index.page.
3. Digital marketing is now re-appropriating the sales budget, Scott Brinker, April 2014; http://chiefmartec.com/2014/04/digital-marketing-now-reappropriating-budget-sales/.

9 A Continuum Fuels Real-Time Relevance

1. Tony Haile, "What You Know about the Web Is Wrong,", Chartbeat, Time.com, March 9, 2014; http://time.com/12933/what-you-think-you-know-about-the-web-is-wrong/.

2. The 2014 B2B Buyer Behavior Survey, DemandGen Report, January 2014; http://www
.demandgenreport.com/industry-resources/research/2508-the-2014-b2b-buyer-
behavior-survey.html#.U1L3xFdyfsI.

10   Creating a Continuum Approach

1. Bob Johnson, "Forget 2014 Marketing Predictions," IDG Connect, February 2014;
accessed April 19, 2014; http://www.idgconnectmarketers.com/forget-2014-marketing
-predictions/.
2. "Define What's Valued Online" The CMO Council, June 6, 2013; http://www
.cmocouncil.org/cat_details.php?fid=264.
3. "Digital Distress: What Keeps Marketers Up at Night?", Adobe, September 2013;
http://blogs.adobe.com/conversations/2013/09/digital-distress-what-keeps-marketers
-up-at-night.html.
4. "Digital Roadblock: Marketers Struggle to Reinvent Themselves," Adobe, March 2014;
http://www.adobe.com/content/dam/Adobe/en/solutions/digital-marketing/pdfs/adobe
-digital-roadblock-survey.pdf.

11   Moving from Campaign to Continuum

1. Investopedia "Marketing Campaign," accessed on April 27, 2014; http://www.investo
pedia.com/terms/m/marketing-campaign.asp.
2. B2B Content Marketing Budgets, Benchmarks and Trends—North America 2014,
Content Marketing Institute and MarketingProfs, September 2013, http://contentmarket
inginstitute.com/wp-content/uploads/2013/10/B2B_Research_2014_CMI.pdf.

12   Get More Value from Investments in Content

1. "Become Customer Obsessed to Gain Competitive Value," Forrester.com, accessed on
May 18, 2014; http://solutions.forrester.com/empowered-customers.
2. "Opt for Business Empowerment," CoreMedia, accessed on May 18, 2014; http://
www.coremedia.com/web-content-management/what-we-offer/coremedia7/online
-manager/-/29524/29524/-/_vb5qvm/-/index.html.

13   Our Brains on Stories—Why Stories Work

1. Greg J. Stephens, Lauren J. Silbert, and Uri Hasson, "Speaker-Listener Neural Coupling
Underlies Successful Communication, Proceedings of the National Academy of Science,
August 2010; http://www.ncbi.nlm.nih.gov/pmc/articles/PMC2922522/.
2. Annie Murphy Paul, "Your Brain on Fiction,", *New York Times*, March 18, 2012; http://
www.nytimes.com/2012/03/18/opinion/sunday/the-neuroscience-of-your-brain-on
-fiction.html.
3. "The Psychology of Storytelling and Empathy Animated," PsyBlog, accessed on May 24,
2014; http://www.spring.org.uk/2014/01/the-psychology-of-storytelling-and-empathy
-animated.php.

14 The Strategic Value of Storytelling

1. B2B Content Marketing Benchmarks, Budgets and Trends 2014, Content Marketing Institute, October 1, 2013; http://contentmarketinginstitute.com/2013/10/2014-b2b -content-marketing-research/.
2. B2B Content Preferences Survey 2014, DemandGen Report, June 2014; http://www .demandgenreport.com/industry-resources/research.html#.U7cFDbH7Heo.
3. Jill Rosen, "Super Bowl Ads: Stories Beat Sex and Humor, John Hopkins Researcher Finds," HUB, accessed on May 24, 2014; http://hub.jhu.edu/2014/01/31/super-bowl -ads.

Section 5 Responsiveness—Your Ability to Sync Up

1. B2B Technology Content Survey Report, Eccolo Media, November 2013; http://eccolo media.digarati.com/,

21 Engaging Diverse Audiences

1. IDG Customer Engagement Study 2013, September 2013; http://www.idgenterprise .com/report/customer-engagement-2013.

22 Establishing Digital Relevance Across Channels

1. "Building Bridges to the Promised Land: Big Data, Attribution and Omni-Channel," The CMO Club and Visual IQ, January 2014; http://www.visualiq.com/cmo-club -study-download-form-web.
2. Ibid.
3. Delivering New Levels of Personalization in Consumer Engagement, Forrester Research, November 2013; https://www.sap.com/bin/sapcom/he_il/downloadasset.2013-11-nov -21-22.delivering-new-levels-of-personalization-in-consumer-engagement-pdf.html.
4. 2013 Market Pulse Survey, Korn Ferry Institute, December 2013; http://www.korn ferryinstitute.com/sites/all/files//documents/briefings-magazine-download/2013%20 Marketing%20Pulse%20Survey.pdf.
5. B2B Content Marketing 2014: Benchmarks, Budgets and Trends—North America, October 2013. http://contentmarketinginstitute.com/2013/10/2014-b2b-content -marketing-research/.
6. "19 Horrific Social Media Fails from the First Half of 2014," eConsultancy, June 2014; https://econsultancy.com/blog/65020-19-horrific-social-media-fails-from-the-first -half-of-2014.
7. Audi #PaidMyDues, accessed July 5, 2014; http://www.audia3presents.com/.
8. The 2014 Professional Content Consumption Report, LinkedIn, June 10, 2014; http://marketing.linkedin.com/blog/announcing-the-2014-professional-content -consumption-report/.

23 Goals—Merging Yours with Theirs

1. "The State of B2B Lead Generation, Buyer Zone," November 2013; http://www.buyer zone.com/leads/resources/state-of-b2b-lead-generation/.

2. Dan Armstrong, "Research Highlight: Marketing Doesn't Know What Buyers Want," ITSMA, January 2014; http://www.itsma.com/ezine/research-highlight-marketing-doesnt-know-what-buyers-want/.

26   Social Advocacy

1. State of the American Consumer, Gallup, June 2014, http://products.gallup.com/171722/state-american-consumer.aspx.

Section 7   Proving Performance—Science, Not Fluff

1. "90% of Marketers Are Not Trained in Marketing Performance and Marketing ROI," Fournaise Marketing Group, April 2014; https://www.fournaisegroup.com/marketers-not-trained-in-marketing-performance-and-roi/.
2. The Converged Campaign Gap, nFusion, December 2013; http://info.nfusion.com/marketing-gap-success

27   Data and Analytics for Business Results

1. Report 2013: Data-Driven Marketing Survey, DOMO, November 2013, http://www.domo.com/learn/2013-data-driven-marketing-survey-report.
2. B2B Content Marketing: Benchmarks, Budgets and Trends 2013, Content Marketing Institute and MarketingProfs, October 2013, http://contentmarketinginstitute.com/2013/10/2014-b2b-content-marketing-research/.

28   Relevance KPIs

1. B2B Content Preferences Survey, DemandGen Report, June 2014; http://www.demandgenreport.com/industry-topics/content-strategies/2746-b2b-content-preferences-survey-buyers-want-short-visual-mobile-optimized-content.html#.U7M5QLH7Heq.

30   Empowering Sales with Content

1. Content Marketing and Sales Effectiveness Survey, Richardson, May 2013; http://www.richardson.com/PageFiles/Articles/content-marketing-sales-effectiveness-survey.pdf.

About the Author

Ardath Albee helps her clients create digital marketing strategies every day that turn prospects into buyers via compelling content and online engagement. She has over 29 years of business management and marketing experience that helps her align marketing programs with business objectives, resulting in quantifiable proof that marketing programs can drive business transformation.

Over the past three years, Ardath has created nearly 100 buyer personas, along with content strategies, that have helped clients, including BMC, CoreMedia, Sykes, Demandbase, Deluxe, Teradata, and Cisco's partners attract, engage, and interactively motivate prospects to become customers.

Ardath is a speaker, storyteller, author, instructor, and marketing strategist, who has been selected as a Top 50 Marketing and Sales Influencer for the last three years. She speaks in person and online at industry conferences, for associations, and for marketing-focused businesses, helping their audiences learn how to share more relevant stories that create intentional and mutually beneficial relationships.

Her first book, *eMarketing Strategies for the Complex Sale*, was published by McGraw-Hill in 2009.

Index